HOW TO SUCCEED IN HIGH SCHOOL AND PREP FOR COLLEGE

Book 1 of How to Succeed in High School, College and Beyond College

By Phyllis Zimbler Miller, M.B.A.

AUTHOR BIO

Phyllis Zimbler Miller has a B.A. in Journalism from Michigan State University and an M.B.A. in Finance from The Wharton School of the University of Pennsylvania. Before getting her M.B.A., she was a newspaper journalist and taught newswriting courses and copyediting courses at Temple University Center City.

She is the co-founder of the Los Angeles-based online marketing company MillerMosaicLLC.com, which is now WBENC certified and works with clients on effectively using social media and other online marketing and branding strategies.

Applying these marketing and branding strategies to the academic arena, Phyllis works with students on their college, law school and medical school applications.

Check out her other projects/books at PhyllisZimblerMiller.com, including:

- HOW TO SUCCEED IN COLLEGE AND PREP FOR BEYOND COLLEGE

- HOW TO SUCCEED BEYOND COLLEGE

TABLE OF CONTENTS

In an ideal world you or your parents, advisors and mentors would be reading this book the summer before you enter ninth grade. Realistically, though, you may already be in 9th, 10th, 11th or even 12th grade when you read this book.

The information on interviews is in Chapter II because this very important information is not only for college admission interviews. The information in Chapter II is important for numerous situations on your way to college admission interviews.

In order to make it easier for you to find the information you want at any particular moment, below is a very complete table of contents.

How should you talk during a meeting or interview?
What about body language during a meeting or interview for an internship, summer job or college admission?
What about interviews conducted online via a chat system?

AFTER A MEETING/INTERVIEW
How important is saying thank you for the meeting or interview?

CHAPTER III: PLANNING AHEAD FOR HIGH SCHOOL

CHOOSING YOUR HIGH SCHOOL COURSES BEFORE SCHOOL BEGINS
What is the big deal about choosing high school courses for all four years before you even start high school?
How do you do this research?
What are you going to be when you grow up?

ADVANCED PLACEMENT COURSES IN HIGH SCHOOL
What is the big deal with AP courses?

THE FUN PART OF HIGH SCHOOL – EXTRACURRICULAR ACTIVITIES
To what do you want to devote your extracurricular time?
What about extracurricular activities in connection with college applications?
How important is doing community service for your college application resume?
Then what is a teen to do?
What about the question of well-rounded or specialist?
Are there ways to stand out in following your passion?
What if you are not a leader?
What is the big deal about making choices?
Is there anything else you should take into account when planning for extracurricular activities?
What about high schools' college counselors?
How do you keep track of all this information you are going to collect?
Anything else of which you should keep track?
And what about those adults to whom you have access? What about alumni interviews?

And what about those adults to whom you have access?

What are some examples of activities for the summer before 12th grade?

ADDITIONAL ASSISTS IN COLLEGE APPLICATIONS
Can sports be a possible assist into college? (Do not automatically skip this section.)
Where can you learn which schools have which college teams?

STANDARDIZED TESTS
A word about the SATs or the ACTs

GET ALL THE INFORMATION YOU CAN ON EACH COLLEGE
Should you attend the local area presentations given by colleges that interest you?

FINANCIAL AID
Where is the money and who qualifies for it?

EXERCISES

CHAPTER V: AFTER THE COLLEGE/PROGRAM APPLICATIONS ARE IN

Is there anything you can do now to enhance your candidacy?
Is there anything else you should be doing in preparation for college or program acceptance?
What about after you have gotten the results?
What might you do during a gap year?
What about transferring?
What if all else fails?

EXERCISES

BONUS: Tips for How to Use Dynamic Language on a College Application Essay

INTRODUCTION: YOUR OWN PATH

Congratulations! You have just graduated from 8th grade.

The next four years ahead look pretty good. Sure, you will have homework and your parents will still be nagging about things like taking out the trash and always wearing your safety belt when you start driving. Yet from your point of view these four years will be FUN, FUN, FUN. You will have more freedom and maybe very little responsibility.

Why bother reading this book now? Can all that thinking about college wait till at least fall semester of senior year of high school?

Start to plan now so you will have an easier path in the future.

Believe it or not, if you start now learning specific skills and planning ahead in certain areas, the path of your life can be much smoother, wherever that path may lead you. And, hey, you might want to get a job or internship during high school. Do you know how to go about doing that?

Follow the advice of this book to get a head start.

And in case you are wondering, the origins of this material come from a long time ago – as far back as the Stone Age may seem to you. Therefore, the explanation about this material is in a NOTE FOR PARENTS, ADVISORS OR MENTORS. Go ahead and show the note to these people.

Good luck on your journey,

Phyllis Zimbler Miller

Beverly Hills, California

NOTE FOR PARENTS, ADVISORS AND MENTORS:

In the fall of 1977 I decided I wanted to get an M.B.A. from Wharton in Philadelphia, where I lived at the time. I knew I did not have much to offer Wharton – I would be 30 when I started Wharton (at a time when most people got an M.B.A. right after undergraduate school); I had not had math since junior year of high school (algebra II at that); and I had not done anything in the business field (I was an editor/reporter at a weekly newspaper). Why would Wharton accept me?

To help my chances, I conducted a marketing campaign for myself: took a pre-calculus course at a local college that demonstrated I could do math and helped with my GMAT score; wrote a bi-weekly "Money Matters" newspaper column that showcased an interest in finance/business; arranged good recommendation letters; had the voluntary on-campus interview. All these activities repositioned me in regard to what I could offer Wharton.

When I applied, I appeared to be a serious candidate for a graduate business degree. And the campaign worked – I was accepted to and graduated from the 1980 Wharton M.B.A. class.

Years later it took some time for me to make the connection between this successful marketing campaign and the goal of my older daughter to get into the college of her choice. When I finally made the connection that applicants to undergraduate college also needed to conduct marketing campaigns, I jumped into the fray to learn as much as possible about the crucial four years of high school leading up to college.

The knowledge I began developing helped both my older and my younger daughter in their college applications. And as I learned more, I realized that this information could be valuable for all high school students.

If you are reading this, I hope you will commit to helping the high school students in your life as they begin their journey to college and beyond.

WARNING – READ THIS RIGHT NOW TO SAVE YOURSELF FROM MAJOR MISTAKES

No matter what – NEVER, EVER, EVER put anything online that could damage your future.

And NEVER believe that privacy controls will protect you. Even if you think no one except yourself can see that nude picture of you, do NOT put it online.

While I am a huge advocate of effectively using social media for your goals in life, I also know that sharing inappropriate information, photos or videos can really hurt you.

In case you are unsure what could be harmful to your college applications or beyond – here is a partial list:

Photos or videos of yourself with beer, alcohol or controlled substances in your hands

Photos or videos of yourself in lewd (or no) clothing

Photos or videos of yourself making vulgar hand gestures

Comments or videos with R-rated swear words

Hurtful comments or videos about others

Photos and comments can live on the Internet forever even if you have deleted these. Please do NOT shoot yourself in the foot by putting inappropriate photos, videos or comments online.

CHAPTER I: TAKING YOUR OWN PATH

Let's answer some relevant questions right now before we explore the most important theme in this whole book.

OPTIONS AND CONTROL

Are you only reading this book because an adult insisted?

I know, I know. You are drowning in homework, learning a new vocabulary word every day for those far-off college admission standardized tests, playing goalie on your high school soccer team, still taking those piano lessons your parents insisted on way back in first grade, etc., etc., etc.

Do you really have to think about preparing for the rest of your life now? Because, honestly, even the thought of applying to college makes you nervous and, thank heavens, it is three years away. And your career path? Light years away!

Let me tell you why it is worth the time and effort to read this NOW:

1) To help ensure you have **options** in your future life – whatever path you may take.

2) To help give you some measure of **control** over your own path.

And, no, these two are not the same.

The first reason enables you to be exposed to different experiences than you might otherwise have undertaken plus learn some important life skills that will stand you in good stead in life.

The second reason will enable you to feel you have some control over the whole process rather than feeling a martyr to this trial-by-fire rite of passage.

What if you are reading this book even though your family wants you not to go away to college?

If your family is not supportive of your desire to go to college, or if your family is supportive but does not know how to help you, you must seek out people who can help you apply to colleges, help you apply for scholarships, and, perhaps most importantly, help convince your family that this path is right and best for you.

For example, you may want to go to college away from home while your family wants you to attend local college. Or you may encounter family discouragement if you want to drop out of college to follow a dream. In both these cases you will need to find people to help support your decision and to give you advice.

Seek out people who can encourage you on your chosen path.

PASSION – THE NUMBER ONE THEME OF THIS BOOK

What do we mean by passion?

Not a romance novel but something you love doing or learning about. And not necessarily a passion that will be yours happily ever after. More likely a passion you would like to explore now. This passion can be anything – it does not have to be career or job-directed at this point. Just something you love doing that is legal!

High school is a good time to start finding your passion.

And what if you change your mind about this passion? You can actually be fickle about passions, as long as you do not take up a new passion every week.

Let's say, for example, you discover after two years of high school, during which you have focused on marine biology, that you realize marine biology is not your thing. Now you can explore a new passion!

And, yes, if we are talking college applications, the official wisdom may be that colleges like to see high school students who have stuck to something and not tried every new fad. Yet trying out two different passions can still demonstrate stick-to-it-ness.

Imagine a student who, for the first two years of high school, works as a volunteer with kids at a marine biology museum. Then at this point she realizes she does not like marine biology yet loves working with kids. The following two years of high school she volunteers in a variety of kid-centered activities to learn more about in what context she likes working with kids.

If this student writes an effective college application essay about what her first two years volunteering at a marine biology museum taught her about herself and her future direction, this could be an impressive example of a student going outside her school to explore her own potential passions and then developing career goals from what she learned about herself.

Your passion is not written in stone.

While it is important to explore a passion during high school, you do **not** have to make a decision in high school about your college major or field of study. Even if you have a passion that you consistently focus on during high school, you can still apply as an undecided major to college.

Nor must you do only activities in that passion. You can do clubs, volunteer, etc. in unrelated areas as long as you demonstrate some passion – one area in which you participate/study more intensely.

Social media tip: The activities you participate in for your passion are usually good ones to share on social media sites such as Facebook and Twitter. You can post, for example, about searching for sea urchins or volunteering as a child's reading tutor.

NOTE FOR PARENTS, ADVISORS AND MENTORS – "MIDWIFE" PASSION

You have the up-close-and-personal opportunity of being a midwife to a teen's passions at this age. If, for example, your fifteen-year-old says he/she wants to option a Young Adult novel as a possible movie project, do not say that the teen is too young to do this. If you know how to go about optioning a book, or know someone who can tell you, help your teen. Even if he/she is not able to option the book, your teen will have had a great learning experience (and one that can be written about for a college application essay or as blog posts or updates on Twitter, Facebook or other social media sites).

Another example: If your teen says he/she wants to be a playwright and wants to start seeing plays, yet the major theater venues in your city charge ticket prices that would break your recreation budget, look into small theaters and community theaters where the ticket prices are lower. Let your aspiring playwright read the reviews and then choose which of these plays to attend with you. (And perhaps your teen can even start writing online reviews of plays.)

A third example: A teenage kid who designs Medieval armor. Instead of complaining about the mess he/she makes with the full-size constructions, try to arrange a specific workshop area. And, for your teen's future portfolio, take pictures of the completed constructions before they disintegrate in the attic or basement. You might even encourage your teen to share these photos online in appropriate social media venues.

The bottom line is that your teen's currently expressed passion may not be a lifelong passion. Yet you want to encourage a teen's search for a passion for two reasons, and only the second is for the college application process. The more important reason is that having a passion in life may lead to more happiness in life. The skills discussed in this book are to be used now and in the future.

Join the passion hunt. And, yes, it helps to take an interest in that passion. You might be amazed how a surly teen who will not talk to you about high school classes or what is happening with friends will be willing to discuss with you the groin protectors on suits of armor or the flying buttresses on Gothic churches. And during the teen years, any time you can have a non-shouting conversation is a good time.

STARTING AT THE BEGINNING – YOUR RESUME

Why do you need a resume now?

It is never too early to start preparing your resume.

Even if you are convinced you will not need a resume for a year or two, start one now. One reason is so that you do not, at a later date, forget some important items, such as that impressive community service project you did during 9th grade. Or you may forget the official title of the local library essay contest you won.

There is a second reason we are discussing this now instead of later in the book. As we go over the items likely to be put on your high school resume, you may be motivated into thinking about specific paths for yourself.

Third reason: IF YOU HAVE A RESUME RIGHT NOW – you will always be ready if someone unexpectedly offers you an internship or summer job opportunity.

Set up a resume document on your computer and then you will be ready to add to it as you go along. I like to call this a "resume-as-you go."

Prepare a "resume-as-you-go," adding information as it happens.

FORMATTING A RESUME

Which format should you follow as everyone has a different suggestion?

Yes, everyone has an opinion about formatting a resume. For example, some people like education listed at the top; some like education listed at the bottom. Some like hobbies included; some do not. Some resumes emphasize accomplishments rather than positions. Research resume advice to choose a format that resonates with you.

When you are starting out it is a good idea to keep your resume to one page with an easily readable type font.

Here are the important points no matter what resume format you use:

1) No spelling or grammar mistakes.

2) Only capitalize proper nouns. If you do not know what this means, see the tip sheet in the next chapter.

3) Have someone unfamiliar with your information read your resume to ensure that everything makes sense.

4) Go for ease of reading above all else – do **not** use several different fonts and other fancy elements that muddy the readability.

5) If you have a passion, there should be items on your resume that indicate this passion.

6) Make sure that the most important information STANDS OUT.

Resumes are written in a special, abbreviated sentence structure.

Resumes are written in partial sentences, so forget about complete sentences starting with "I was." In a resume there is no need to say: I was a lab assistant at a radiation laboratory. Instead you can list the name of the lab, then a dash, and then the words assistant or lab assistant. Under that line of information you write a brief description (see below.) Since it is your resume, it is clear that it is you who performed the research experiments.

Universal Lab – Assistant

January-March 2011, Los Angeles

Performed research experiments on rats to determine the missing gene that may lead to a cure for Alzheimer's under the supervision of the head of the biogenetics department.

And choose strong action words that convey positive images – performed is one such word. This is much better than saying, for example: Did research experiments. Of course you did them. Performed, conducted, etc. are stronger words. Use specific visual images that catch the attention of the person reading your resume.

Use specific words to create more opportunities for discussion.

Your goal is to prompt discussion from your resume that can establish rapport in an interview. Here is an example of this:

My younger daughter listed on her resume that she had done research at a film production company internship. The research had been rather unusual – on the 15th century "Malleus Maleficarum" written for Pope Innocent VIII on witchcraft trials – although she did not include this information on her resume. She later revised her resume to include this specific info about the "Malleus Maleficarum." At the very next interview she had, this item on her resume prompted a friendly discussion because the interviewer had been reading about Popes. (She got the job – although probably not because of the research.)

Below is an example of a resume for a fictional student in spring semester of her senior year of high school. Can you spot the student's passion?

CHARLENE STUDENT
101 Cherry Lane * Smalltown, CA 90212
310-555-1234 * charlene.student@gmail.com

EDUCATION:
SMALLTOWN HIGH SCHOOL

September 2007 – Present, Smalltown

UCLA EXTENSION, "Intro to Advertising"

Fall Quarter 2010, Los Angeles

WORK EXPERIENCE:

STARBUCKS – Barista

November 2010 – Present, Los Angeles

Perform counter duties and other tasks as needed. Participate in frequent customer service training.

SUNSHINE DAY CARE CENTER – Aide

Summer 2010, Smalltown

Responsible for assisting child care supervisor. Took on-site CPR training.

INTERNSHIP EXPERIENCE:

STAR ADVERTISING AGENCY – Intern

Summer 2010, Los Angeles

Assisted in media buying department. Responsible for tracking buys on national television and social media sites.

SMALLTOWN NEWSPAPER – Intern

March-May 2010, Los Angeles

Worked in ad department charting promotion response rates.

VOLUNTEER EXPERIENCE:

HABITAT FOR HUMANITY – Worker   December 2009, New Orleans

Helped build homes in New Orleans with LA church group.

SMALLTOWN SENIOR CENTER – Entertainer

Summer 2009, Smalltown

Performed musical theater show tunes for center residents.

HIGH SCHOOL ACTIVITIES:

Student Council Representative	9, 10, 11, President–12
Intramural Volleyball	11, 12
French Club	9, 10, 11, 12
Model U.N.	12
High School Newspaper (Ad Department)	9, 10, 11, 12

Because this sample student is a senior in high school, I have put her education at the top of the resume. If she attends college – during the years she is still in college she may continue to put her education at the top (replacing her high school listing with the college she is currently attending). In this way an interviewer can quickly see she has not yet graduated. After she graduates college and has her first post-college job, she may want to move her education information to the end of her resume.

Be careful of the words you use to describe what you have done. The first work experience listing as a barista at Starbucks starts out with the present-tense verb **perform** because that job is currently being done. The second item as an aide at the Sunshine Day Care Center uses the word **responsible**, which is correct either for past tense or present tense – "I am responsible" or "I was responsible." (In this case the word is being used in connection with a job in the past.) The third item has the past-tense verb **assisted** because that job was done in the past.

And the student's passion in the above sample resume is -- advertising.

Check out her resume to see how many of the resume items support this passion. And she could talk about her passion in an email or in an interview.

Social media tip: If she has been on Facebook since she turned 13 and thus of legal age (by Facebook's terms of service) to join the social media site, she may have been posting updates about her various experiences. These updates may have helped her get her paid and volunteer opportunities.

Make clear the important points of your resume.

What about an example of a different format for a resume?

Here is an explanation of a student's most important points in a different resume format than the sample resume above:

A student entering senior year of high school originally listed all his activities in three sections with the following boldface headings: **junior year, sophomore year, freshman year**. In order to figure out how many years the student had undertaken each activity, an interviewer would have to search each section for the information. What is more, the boldface headings were wasted on meaningless information – the year in school.

The student redesigned his one-page resume to make the important information stand out. Under the overall heading ACTIVITIES he listed these sections in boldface: **clubs, community service, political camps, honors, writing, sports, performing arts**. Just by reading down these boldface subheads, an interviewer could get a quick picture of the student's interests. Then a closer read would reveal the years of these activities, etc.

In addition, the student placed his superior SAT scores and GPA at the top of his resume rather than tucking this information as an afterthought at the bottom of his resume. Now he had a much stronger visual representation of his interests and his strengths.

WHAT GOES ON A RESUME

Do you have to put everything on your resume?

Including your standardized test scores or GPA is up to you.

You decide whether you want to put your standardized scores and/or GPA on your resume. If you think this can help, go ahead. Remember, you can choose what to put on your resume as long as it is the truth.

Always tell the truth on your resume – Big Brother is watching.

The universe is perverse, and if you tell a lie on your resume, the one person who knows about the lie may talk to the person you are trying to impress with the lie. And with everyone's access today to the Internet, the discovery of the lie may only be a click away.

Social media tip: Be careful if you complain online about grades you got. You never know who might have seen the complaint. This is a topic probably best discussed only offline.

Now the advertising plug for this book: If in 9th grade you start following the suggestions in this book, you will be well prepared for filling out your college applications **and you will not be tempted due to desperation to lie on the applications.**
If you follow the suggestions here, you will not be shocked to suddenly learn – when it is too late – that colleges ask about your community-service activities, your passions, what you have done outside of school, your job history (paid and unpaid). Throughout your high school years – by engaging in activities that truly interest you – you will be working towards being able to fill out these applications with meaningful information.

It is okay to brag on your resume -- you want to look good.

What things can you leave off your resume?

Put your best foot forward.

You can leave off from your resume things that are not important to your overall profile. If, for example, you had a summer job only for two weeks because it did not work out, you do not have to list it on your resume. It adds nothing to the overall picture of your abilities and interests. What you decide to put on your resume, as long as it is accurate, is up to you.

And, remember, **a resume needs to be updated** even if you think nothing is new. Plan to check your resume every couple of months while you are in the process of college applications to ensure everything is current.

For extra help in organizing material for your resume, look at the work sheet for developing a college application resume at the end of this chapter. While this work sheet has some information categories not needed for a regular resume (such as your place of birth), the work sheet will give you an idea of some of the items you might include on your college application information.

What about putting your resume online?

Be very careful if you post your resume online.

NEVER put your social security number on your resume whether posting online to a job search website or emailing to someone or handing your resume to someone. And when posting online, you probably want to withhold your street address and other information until you have a face-to-face interview.

Social media tip: Also consider what information you put on social media sites such as Facebook. You want to keep both privacy/security concerns and your overall image in mind at all times.

Do you have to keep records of all your activities during high school?

While it is very important to keep a running resume so that you will remember everything, it is equally important to keep paperwork from those activities as proof that you have actually done them.

A University of California, Berkeley freshman was asked to provide proof within a very short time frame of all the summer classes she had listed on her resume. This list included a three-week non-credit high school writing course held at UCLA and taken before her freshman year of high school. Luckily she had saved the assignments, on which she found the teacher's name. Then she was able to contact the teacher, who agreed to verify that the course had been taken.

In order to avoid such complications:

For each activity keep registration slips, final reports, assignments, emails from soccer coaches, competition results, etc. clipped together by activity in a high school resume folder or in an online file. Then if you are called upon to provide proof of something, the information will be easily available.

Keep paperwork proof of all your high school activities.

Work Sheet for Developing a College Application Resume

Here is a work sheet to assist you to consider the potential areas of interest to a college admission office.

Education (when applying for internships, jobs, etc. – probably not necessary on college applications where high school listed elsewhere)

Internships (paid or unpaid)

Community service

Work experience (paid -- although if no paid work experience, consider putting community service experience under this category if appropriate experience)

Courses taken at other schools or colleges or other activities demonstrating academic pursuits outside the student's school

Extracurricular activities (within and outside school)

Honors/awards/achievements

Recent camp/travel

Athletics

Special interests/abilities

Languages spoken at home (if other than English)

Place of birth

Place of mother's birth

Place of father's birth

People who will provide recommendations (besides teachers and high school college counselor)

Hardships overcome (this is a tricky area and must be carefully considered before revealing)

Unique promise (what do you uniquely promise the college that you will bring to the table if you are accepted)

Coming next: Preparing for interviews or meetings.

CHAPTER II: PREPARING FOR INTERVIEWS OR MEETINGS

As we talk about certain skills, I am going to use the word **interview** or **meeting** interchangeably. You may have a meeting only for information purposes – an informational – or you may have an interview for an internship or a summer job or college admissions. Whatever the specific purpose for meeting or communicating with adults who may hold a key to your future, the things we are going to now discuss will apply.

GENERAL PREPARATIONS FOR YOUR LIFE PATH

Does the Internet's instant global access affect what you do?

Google yourself. Then check for skeletons in the closet.

Social media tip: Thanks to the Internet anything can come back to bite you – and probably will. Whatever you post on YouTube, Facebook or any of the other social media sites may possibly be seen by anyone regardless of the supposed privacy controls! Even professional networking sites such as LinkedIn can have risks to your reputation.

Keep your act clean – Big Brother is watching!

If you are contemplating pranks such as stealing the high school's flagpole, think again. It probably sounds like a lot of fun now, but do you really want to explain to a prospective summer job employer why your picture is on the front page of your local newspaper under the headline "Vandal Steals School Property"?

Loose lips sink ships.

The above saying was coined during time of war as a warning not to give away military secrets to the enemy. Today it is a saying that can stand you in good stead in numerous situations.

For example, while only you can hear the person's words on the other end of your cell phone conversation, anyone and everyone can hear what you say if you are in a public place. And you might be surprised what people can figure out from hearing only one side of a conversation. There is another saying: Better safe than sorry. If you remember this second saying in connection with the loose lips saying above, you should be in good shape. And whenever you are in public, whether on or off your phone, be careful of what you say.

Can you use any email address that you like?

Have a cute email address? Get a professional one.

If your email address is some cute handle, keep it for your friends. And immediately get a new professional-sounding email address for college applications, internships, recommendation requests. Trust me, copycat@domain.com is not likely to inspire confidence in a college admissions officer. Nor will bigmouth@domain.com help get you a summer job.

Use your own name as your email address.

Using your name as your email address is professional and reminds people each time they see the email that it is from you. (Most businesses use some form of a person's name as his/her email address.)

If you have a cute email address, you may have to write in the subject line "From Phyllis Miller" in order to ensure that the email recipient will open your email. This is not cool because:

a) You have blown your chance to have a strong subject line that hooks the recipient into reading the email right now.

b) The recipient could find your cute email address offensive in some way unbeknownst to you.

Keep copycat@domain.com or bigmouth@domain.com for your pals if you must, and get a professional email address such as John.Doe@domain.com for all professional correspondence.

Pothole alert: Any email may be seen by the world as it is easy to forward email to others. Only put into an email what you are willing for others – any others – to read.

Tell sensitive info to people by phone; not voicemail, email or texting.

And be very careful if you receive an email with several recipients: If you are replying, make sure you click the **reply** button and NOT the **reply all** button if your reply is intended only for the recipient and not for all the others.

Are there other suggestions for setting up professional email and phone communication?

Consider a separate email account for all your important emails.

After you have gotten an email with your name – consider getting a separate email account, for example, for all your college admissions email communication. Then when you are in a hurry, you may just check the account with the email address you are using for this communication.

If you decide to do this, it probably would be better to have a separate address at a different domain rather than a different version of your name at the same domain. If the college admissions email address is so close to the original one at the same domain (perhaps with or without your middle initial), you may mix up your two accounts when giving out your email address.

Have a professional-sounding message on your voicemail.

Imagine an interviewer calls you and is greeted with this voicemail message: "Hey, I'm out doing something possibly illegal but I'll get back to you if I don't go to jail." Or what about an interviewer having to wait through two minutes of a hip hop song? What are the odds the caller will hang around long enough to leave a message?

Instead go with a short, professional message that lets the caller know that he/she has reached the correct person and number: "You have reached (your name) at (telephone number). Please leave a message." If you want to add something upbeat, you could say something such as: "I look forward to speaking with you."

Are there guidelines for getting back to people who offer to help?

Always promptly respond to an email or call offering to help you.

For example, if someone offers to help you and gives you her/his email address to send your resume, you should immediately email your resume. (You should always have your resume ready to go if you have been following the advice in this book.)

If you do not send your resume immediately, you risk appearing not to be that interested in the offered help. And if you are not that interested, why should the person who offered to help you be interested in helping?

Always immediately reply to a networking connection offer.

Even if you are unsure whether to accept an offer of help, immediately reply thanking the person for the offer of help, explaining you are still undecided, and ending by saying you will get back in touch with the person if you decide to pursue the offer.

It is as simple as this example:

Kathy:

Thank you so much for your offer to help me with finding a summer

20

internship. At this time I have not yet decided what I plan to do for the summer. If I decide to move forward with this type of internship, I will contact you.

Regards,
High School Student

Let people know if you will be offline.

If you know that you will not be able to be online for several days (for whatever reason), say so upfront. Here is an example: "Thank you so much for your offer to help. I'll be offline until next Monday, at which time I'll email you."

This way, when the person offering to help does not hear from you for several days, he/she will not be annoyed that you did not immediately follow up on an offer to help.

***Social media tip:** Yes, although you may be away from a computer, you may have your phone with you and be able to text someone. I do **not** recommend you text to a professional contact. First, the person may not want to receive a text from you to his/her phone. Second, you risk spelling and grammar mistakes that can impact negatively on you. (Personally, I am not very impressed by the message on a text that says to forgive errors because the message was texted.)*

What are effective telephone communication skills?

Effective telephone communication is a skill that must be learned.

Even in a world of email, texting, and social media sites, much of your contact with people in the adult world who might help you will be on the telephone. And this phone connection is often the first time a person "meets" you.

Remember to smile when you speak on the phone.

Even though the other person cannot see your smile, this physical act increases the pleasantness of your voice. If you do not believe this, try it out on your friends. See if they can tell the difference as to when you are smiling and when you are not.

Introduce yourself by name while speaking clearly and slowly.

After saying your name, immediately ask if the other person has time to talk or would it be better to call back at another time. If the reply is to call back, ask when that better time would be. (And, of course, call back at that time.)

How long is appropriate before returning a professional phone call or email?

Although some calls and emails require a higher priority and prompter response than others, let's look at an example of a good return policy:

If someone leaves a phone message or emails you to set up an interview, it would be a good idea to return that message/email as soon as possible after you receive it – definitely the same day.

If you call someone back and do not reach him/her, leave a polite message, including when is a good time for you to be reached. You could also leave your email address – spoken very clearly – on a phone message, offering it as an alternative to another return phone call.

Check your email and voicemail several times each day.

If you are engaged in professional communication, check your voicemail and email several times a day and then respond promptly. (If you are going to be away from email access for several days, you might consider having an automatic reply sent to people who email you. The automatic reply would explain you are away from email access until a specific date.)

Are there tips for effective emails?

Absolutely.

First, you want to make it as easy as possible for someone to decide to open your email. (Many people get dozens of emails a day and do not open all of them.)

Second, you want to make it as easy as possible for the person to read your email, understand your request, and act on it.

In order to achieve both of these goals:

1)   Always write a subject in the subject line (why should anyone bother to open an email with no subject?) and the more specific the better, such as "College recommendation request from a former student" rather than "Hello."

2)   Use correct spelling, grammar and punctuation. Do NOT write: "tonite i hope to meet u" and sign with a smiley face. DO write: "Tonight I hope to meet you" and sign your full name.

3)   Do NOT write run-on sentences. These are sentences that may be technically correct yet are way too long for the eye to read comfortably in an email message. After you have written the email, go back and check whether you can make two sentences out of a very long sentence.

4)   Write in short paragraphs, thereby providing white space for the eye so that the text is not too intimidating. Even if you first write everything in one paragraph, go back and break up a long block of text into several paragraphs. Too much dense text can make someone decide not to read your email – or not to read it carefully. **Recommendation:** Again for ease of reading, double space between each paragraph.

5)   If there are several steps or points to the information you are providing, list the points separately, thereby providing white space around each step or point. (Just as I have done here to make this information clearer.) This formatting helps the reader realize that there are several steps or points rather than one huge clump of information.

6)   After you have written the email and run spell check, read the email aloud. Did you leave out any words? Did you use the words

you meant to use or did you jumble some words? Did you ask specifically what your request is or did you leave it up to the person to figure out what you are asking? (You must specifically ask for your request; do not assume the email recipient is a mind reader.) Is there a better way to ask your request? If so, revise your email. Yes, I know this is only an email. Yet you might be surprised how important only an email can be to your future. If you want someone to take the time to act on a request from you, take the time to write the request in the best possible way.

7) If you say the person can call you, be sure to include in the email your phone number (and possibly the best hours to reach you if you are in school during the day).

Perhaps the most important tip: When you begin an email, put the subject in the subject line but do NOT put in the email address of whom you are writing. Wait until your entire email is written, spell checked, read aloud and YOU HAVE ATTACHED ANY ATTACHMENTS before you put in the email address. If you follow this rule, you will not be embarrassed by an email accidentally sent before it has been proofread and the attachments attached.

Put in the email address after everything is proofed and attached.

Is good grammar really important in professional communication?

Get a grammar buddy if you need help with good grammar.

If grammar is not your thing, then make it your thing with the help of a friend because a computer's grammar check is not always correct. Have your grammar buddy check all your important emails and applications. And work on learning the correct grammar for the problem areas your grammar buddy discovers you have.

Yes, texting uses symbols and abbreviated spellings. Yet when you are emailing someone in the business world, your grammar and spelling should be as close to perfect as you can make it.

My older daughter heads a management/production film and tv company. Her most frequent complaint: Why should she spend her limited time reading a script whose writer did not take the time to correct the spelling and grammar? And you cannot rely only on spell check and grammar check. It takes a real person looking for errors to catch some of the most obvious mistakes.

Here is a handy tip sheet:

TIP SHEET FOR ELIMINATING PROSIBBLY 50% OF GRAMMAR, SPELLING & PUNCTUATION MISTAKES

(AFTER running spell check, use these rules to catch mistakes spell check does not catch.)

Know the difference between:

1) **their/they're/there**

   Their faces lit up with anticipation. (their – possessive)

   They're waiting for you. (they are – subject and verb)

   The car is over there. (location)

2) **your/you're**

   Your face is sparkling. (your – possessive)

   You're always right. (you are – subject and verb)

3) **it's/its**

   It's nice of you to visit. (it is – subject and verb)

   Jane put on her coat. Its buttons shone. (it – possessive but NO apostrophe)

Know when to use apostrophes:

The passenger's seat was uncomfortable. The passengers' seats were uncomfortable. (possessive singular and possessive plural– use apostrophe)

The passengers were uncomfortable. (plural noun – no apostrophe)

In English, only proper nouns are capitalized:

The Los Angeles County Museum of Art is a terrific museum.

I often visit the art museum.

In direct address, commas set off the name of the person being addressed:

Yes, John, I am going to the movie. Dan, are you going with John?

Recommended stylebook: The Elements of Style by William Strunk Jr. and E.B. White

For extra credit: If you are truly committed to using the correct word appropriately (and you should be truly committed), get Nancy Ragno's book "Word Savvy: Use the Right Word Every Time, All the Time" published by Writer's Digest Books. See especially the chapter "Master 76 Commonly Confused Word Pairs" and the chapter "Conquer 52 Commonly Misused Words." This is definitely my kind of book!

Is it important to use active verbs in essay writing?

Use active verbs when possible, especially in essay writing.

Though I used a passive verb in "the passengers were" in an example above, using an active verb would be more interesting in an essay: The hard seats of the wagon coach caused the passengers to fidget as they tried for a more comfortable position. (Yes, this is a much longer sentence. Remember, though, here we are talking about essay writing and not emails.)

High school English teachers are big on giving this advice about active verbs, which may seem like extra work to you. Yet if you want to write effective essays to enter writing competitions, for example, and for college applications or for effective emails for internships or summer jobs, you will pay attention to **showing** through active verbs rather than **telling** through passive verbs.

Is how you sound when you speak really important?

Work on your accent if people have trouble understanding you.

Most of us born in the U.S. have some kind of regional accent. These accents can often be quite appealing as can some foreign accents. Sometimes, however, an accent can work against you either by the image the accent conveys or in making it difficult for others to understand you.

When I worked at a newspaper office years ago, we had an intern with that particularly grating Philadelphia accent. (It is hard to describe this accent – basically it consists of mispronouncing words in a very grating manner.) The other reporters laughed at her accent behind the intern's back.

I called the intern into my office and suggested that, if she wanted to get ahead in journalism, perhaps she should work on her accent. Her reply: "My parents think my accent is fine but my boyfriend says it's awful." I gently told her that her boyfriend, not her parents, were correct. She needed to lose her particular Philadelphia accent.

Get help for improving your accent if it is bothersome.

How to get help for an unappealing accent? First, voice pronunciation programs are available for actors to eliminate their troublesome accents. You can get such programs from a store catering to actors (such as Samuel French) or from a library to practice on your own or do an online search to find help. (Type "eliminate foreign accent" or "eliminate regional accent" on Google and you will get several websites.)

Second, you can find a friend with the accent you would like to have and practice how the friend speaks. The friend can record troublesome words and sentences so that you can practice on your own.

(When I worked with native French speaker Angelique Glennon for the program "Understand French Like a Native – www.UnderstandFrenchLikeaNative.com – we practiced her English together before recording her English explanations and French pronunciations. While she is fluent in English, her pronunciation of certain English words sometimes sounds more French than English.)

Additional tip: There are other voice issues besides an unpleasant accent. If you feel that your speaking voice is not as good as it could be, consider taking voice (speaking) lessons or finding other ways to practice your public speaking (being interviewed is "public speaking").

Should you ignore possible learning issues you have and just accept that is how you are?

Get help when you need it.

Many students have difficulties that are recognized or diagnosed in elementary school. Yet, for some students, the realization that extra help is needed in test taking or concentrating techniques or any of a number of other concerns does not crop up until the high school years. At this point students may feel too self-conscious to get help in order to discover what is going on and what coping skills can be used.

For those of you who feel that something is interfering with your learning effectiveness, yet you are not ready to ask your school for help, do an online search for books and blogs that may speak to you. When you have found information that resonates with your issues, you may be better prepared to seek out help.

Doing the research to find the help you need.

One such organization for reading help can be found at http://www.learningally.org/ And thanks to the proliferation of ebook readers, tablets, etc. – many with read-aloud sound options, students with reading difficulties have more and more help available.

BEFORE A MEETING/INTERVIEW

Now it is time to consider getting ready for meetings or interviews. The first thing to think about is:

What do you wear?

Dress up rather than down if you are unsure what to wear.

There are numerous information sources that go into detail about how you should dress for various situations. If you are interviewing for an internship or summer job, do your research on the particular company and/or profession when deciding what to wear to an interview or meeting. Different occupations have different looks for the workplace.

If you are interviewing in connection with college admissions, you might call the admissions office and ask specifically what is recommended. If you cannot find out, do dress up rather than down.

The term "dress" includes clean and appropriate **clothing**, clean and appropriate **hair** (including well-trimmed beards), clean and appropriate **fingernails**, and minimal make-up. Also, no sandals or flip-flops unless you are applying for a beach lifeguard job. (In summer, women's professional sandals may be an exception to this advice about no sandals.) Make sure your shoes are polished and your heels are not run-down. Leave all excessive jewelry at home – especially your nose, tongue or eyebrow rings.

Know what to do about multiple earrings and visible tattoos.

For most colleges it might be a good idea to go with these recommendations regarding earrings and visible tattoos – for other interviews also if you do not know the dress code:

For females only one (or at the most two) earrings per ear. For males no earrings unless you know for sure (having done your research) that this will not negatively impact on the impression you hope to make.

And if you have **tattoos** – wear clothing that covers them unless you know that tattoos are considered very appropriate by the person with whom you are meeting.

Social media tip: For your Facebook profile photo, your Twitter profile photo, your Google Plus profile photo, your LinkedIn profile photo, etc., it would be a good idea to follow these recommendations for earrings and tattoos. In addition, do not use a photo of you showing a low neckline that could be considered provocative. These social media sites are for making connections; there are other sites for dating.

No smell of any kind – neither body odor nor perfume/cologne.

Yes, there should be no smell of any kind. Besides use of unscented deodorant along with soap and water to prevent unpleasant smells, there should be a total absence of any smell because many people are allergic to cologne and perfume. Before a meeting leave off using any cologne, perfume or aftershave. In other words, no smells at all, including no perfumed soaps.

In addition, use a mirror to practice wearing a smile as you talk. You want to make sure your face is pleasant to look at when you are meeting with people. This way they will remember you as an upbeat person.

What else do you need to do to be ready for an interview or meeting?

People are always impressed when you take notes at a meeting.

Before a meeting print out clean copies of your current resume. Have more than one copy with you as the person you are meeting may have asked other people to join the meeting.

When you meet with anyone for an informational meeting for college admission or an internship/summer job interview, you must bring a pad and pen or a tablet to take notes (a laptop may seem too much). You demonstrate that you are interested in what the person has to say by taking notes of his/her important points.

Strive to have a reputation as a dependable person.

If you are expected for an interview or meeting and at the very last minute cannot make it due to a very good reason (and not that your friend asked you to go to a movie), CALL THE APPROPRIATE PERSON AND SAY YOU WILL NOT BE THERE. At the same time ask about rescheduling, so the person knows you are still interested in meeting. (This requires being prepared by getting the phone number of the person with whom you are meeting "just in case.")

Note: I highly recommend that you try NOT to have to reschedule a meeting. Instead, carefully choose the first meeting date so that you do not unintentionally schedule a meeting you later cannot keep.

Always be on time. Err on the early side.

Be on time for an informational meeting or interview. Get there early for coffee or tea around the corner or sit in the outer office before your appointment – you might be amazed what you can learn just by listening to the receptionist.

If you have given yourself plenty of extra time and yet are unexpectedly detained (Martians have landed on the highway on which you are driving), **call ahead and say you will be late**. People do **not** recommend or hire anyone who is undependable.

DURING A MEETING/INTERVIEW

When does the meeting or interview actually begin?

Everything you do from the moment you arrive at a meeting/interview location may be observed and noted. This could be something as unexpected as the parking attendant noticing how dirty your car is to the receptionist noticing you read The Wall Street Journal or Popular Mechanic while in the waiting room.

Discard your chewing gum before you arrive at an interview, pop a breath freshener into your mouth, and turn off your cell.

Treat everyone from receptionist to CEO with the same courtesy and respect. (**Please** and **thank you** go a long way.) This is both the correct way to act towards others and you may be saving yourself from making a huge blunder. Who knows if the temporary receptionist is actually the son of the CEO? And guess into whose ear he pours the information on how rudely you acted?

How should you talk during a meeting or interview?

Like, you know, lose these excess words.

The three words "like" and "you know" (along with the annoying "um" and "well") used liberally throughout your conversations may not bother your friends. Yet be assured that a person interviewing you will note the immature and/or annoying language. Other words that bother interviewers include **dude, hey, stuff, whatever**.

And, of course, you should use proper English and not street or slang or colloquial English. If you are not used to answering questions and asking them in proper English – practice, practice, practice with someone who can help you.

Pause before speaking instead of saying "um" or "well."

If necessary when practicing, press your lips firmly together to remind yourself not to say "um" or "well." It is certainly appropriate to take a couple of nanoseconds to think before answering a question.

Speak neither too fast nor too slow.

And consider your volume – how soft or loud – compared to the volume of the person to whom you are talking. If that person speaks in a loud voice, then a soft voice on your part may not be the best strategy. On the other hand, a person who speaks softly (yet clear enough to be heard) may not appreciate your roaring in his/her ear.

Some people make the mistake of lifting their voice at the end of sentences so they sound as if they are asking a question when in fact they are making a statement. That is confusing for the listener.

Others drop their voice so softly at the end of sentences that the final words are difficult to hear

And here is the biggest problem with this particular habit – in effective oral and written communication, the most important words are often and usually should be at the end of the sentence. If those words at the end of your sentence cannot be heard, you have hurt your own presentation.

Your facial expression should match your voice tone. If you are saying something pleasant your expression should match. If you are expressing your anger, you should not confuse signals by smiling. Of course in an interview you are going to control your anger, which is why it is important to practice fielding fast balls from a hostile interviewer.

What about body language during a meeting or interview for an internship, summer job or college admission?

Good posture, direct eye contact, firm handshakes.

As you walk into a room to be interviewed, your posture can make or break you along with a weak or wet handshake, no eye contact, and all the other things your parents have nagged you about for years. (This includes bad table manners – especially a problem when being interviewed at a lunch or dinner.)

Pothole alert: If there are two or more people meeting with you, even if only one person does the talking, you must make and retain your eye contact with all the people present.

Walk into a room with confidence and maintain eye contact throughout the conversation. If you let your eyes roam around the person's office while he/she talks to you, you have probably blown your chances for having made a positive impression.

One exception: If, as you enter the room, you notice out of the corner of your eye, for example, a specific art collection, you may mention this while looking directly into the eyes of the interviewer and shaking hands. For example, you might say "What a lovely collection of penguins you have in your office." This comment shows that you have noticed something specific about the interviewer but you have not done so while he/she is speaking to you while seated at his/her desk.

33

Keep your body still while focusing on the interviewer(s).

During an interview, keep your hands from playing with your hair, your moustache, your pen, the lint on your clothes or rubbing a hangnail. You can lean slightly forward towards the person interviewing you. This subtly conveys that you are truly interested in what the interviewer is saying.

Pothole alert: In Dawn Rosenberg McKay's book "The Everything Practice Interview Book," the author warns there are some people who do not like to shake hands. McKay recommends that you be ready to shake the interviewer's hand when you meet the interviewer but do not offer your hand first. The same goes for the end of the interview when taking your leave. According to McKay, you should keep your right hand free at your side both at the beginning and end of the interview so that you can quickly move your hand into the handshake position if the interviewer offers his/her hand. This excellent piece of advice means that you carry your resumes, purse or briefcase in your left hand in order to keep your right hand free.

McKay also says that the several copies of a resume you bring with you, even if you have sent your resume ahead of time, should be carried in a folder to keep the resumes clean and neat. She also advises: "Women should not carry large, bulky handbags or anything that looks better suited for a day at the beach. No one should carry a backpack, and shopping bags are definitely out."

Check out her book for a helpful section on etiquette when being interviewed during a meal. She has great suggestions for avoiding sand traps as well as avoiding spaghetti sauce on your clothes.

Be careful what your body language signals.

Slumping in a chair can signal you are not serious about the interview. Crossed arms can be perceived as threatening. Fidgeting with your hands conveys nervousness. One leg over the other at the knee appears awkward. If male, keep both feet on the floor. If female, you can cross your legs AT THE ANKLE. Both males and females should strive for body language that shows you are at ease AND giving the interviewer your complete attention.

Of course there will be times when the person with whom you are meeting makes you so uncomfortable that you cannot wait to get out of the room. You should still strive not to show your irritation. Then once you are safely away from the interview, you can treat yourself to a latte or take deep yoga breaths or go for a run or whatever you do to banish such unpleasant experiences. (**Caution:** Do NOT tweet what a lousy experience it was and name names. In fact, it is better not to tweet about this even without naming names. The tweet can reflect badly on you – and the world is watching!)

What about interviews conducted online via a chat system?

Have you heard of speed networking or speed interviewing in person? Imagine speed networking or speed interviewing via an online chat system. Here is how you can prepare ahead of time for such an online chat interview:

Type out some well-thought-out answers to questions an interviewer is likely to ask you. Use these when appropriate to speed up the conversation by copying and pasting the answers from your Word doc.

Do the same thing for questions – prepare some well-thought-out ones. This way you will again appear professional – and you will have time to correct any spelling or typing errors.

Ask about internships. Often unpaid internships are a way to learn about career paths without asking someone for a paying job.

If there is a warning that your quick online chat interview with someone is about to end, express appreciation for the opportunity. People enjoy being thanked for their time and input.

Start practicing now to be able to quickly and accurately type with all your fingers (not just your thumbs on a smartphone).

And while you can have a generic "prep sheet" as a foundation for online interviews, you should add specific answers and questions relating to a specific position before having the interview for that position online. You want to always come across as professional and engaging – not amateurish and blah!

AFTER A MEETING/INTERVIEW

How important is saying thank you for the meeting or interview?

You must immediately email or write a thank-you note (do NOT text) to anyone with whom you have just had a meeting or who talks with you on the phone to give you advice. The person who met with you or spoke to you deserves an immediate email thank-you or handwritten thank-you note even though you have presumably thanked the person for his/her time at the end of the meeting or the phone conversation.

Yes, a thank-you email is probably okay. Yet if you want to stand out in a positive light, and that is what this book is about, write a handwritten note on good stationery or on an appropriate card. That you took the time to do this will impress most interviewers.

To really make an impression -- messenger or drop off a handwritten note.

Remember, whether you write an email or a thank-you note, use proper spelling, grammar and punctuation. And forget about using numerous exclamation points, email symbols, uncapitalized Is, cute spellings (such as u for you). Use formal grammar and NOT texting grammar.

Coming next: Planning for high school.

CHAPTER III: PLANNING AHEAD FOR HIGH SCHOOL

CHOOSING YOUR HIGH SCHOOL COURSES BEFORE SCHOOL BEGINS

The summer of 8th grade is an important time in your future path. Many teens may not know this, but whatever courses you take starting in 9th grade can make your path easier or much more difficult.

What is the big deal about choosing high school courses for all four years before you even start high school?

The early bird catches the worm.

This next section we are going to discuss will require some detective work on the part of you and your parents, advisors or mentors. Or you can get a group of friends together to each take different topics and then pool your researched info. Today, with the ease of the Internet, this vital detective work has never been easier.

Find out the information that high schools do not tell you.

To demonstrate how important it is to do your research BEFORE you start 9th grade, let's discuss one example of the need to be in the know:

Pothole alert: When you start planning what courses you will take for your four years of high school, you may know what your own high school requires (for example, how many years of science, math and a foreign language in order to graduate high school). Equally important, **you may NOT know what courses (and for how many years) colleges will want to see on your high school transcript.**

Your high school may only require three years of math OR completing pre-calculus. On the other hand, a top college may frown on an applicant who has not taken four years of math regardless of whether pre-calculus was completed in junior year or senior year of high school.

Why is this a big deal now? Could you learn this during junior year and just take another year of math in senior year?

Here is what could happen to you:

I know several high school students not especially strong in math who pushed themselves into geometry in 9th grade rather than sticking with algebra that year. Then to their horror they discovered in their junior year – while taking pre-calculus and believing this was the end of their high school math career – they had to take calculus in senior year in order to have the four years of math the top colleges wanted. Yes, calculus because that was the only fourth-year math course available based on what math courses they had already taken!

Many top colleges want to see four years of high school math.

If math is not your strongpoint, it may be better for your high school grade point average if you stick with algebra in 9th grade, geometry in 10th grade, algebra II/trigonometry in 11th grade, and then take pre-calculus in senior year as your fourth year of math. And as an added plus to sticking with algebra in 9th grade, you should then have a stronger grasp of the fundamentals of higher math. Do your own due diligence about math courses in order to make an informed decision. Math is definitely one academic area that can become a pothole on your college applications.

If you want to avoid this pothole and other potential potholes during your high school years, **do your homework the summer before 9th grade** – with the help of others – to find out the high school requirements of those colleges and post-high school programs you might later consider.

How do you do this research?

Yes, this research will take some planning to accomplish. To begin with, check out the websites of the programs and colleges that might interest you in three years. The problem may be that such detailed information – for example, how many years of high school math a top college wants – may not be easily found on the college's website.

Another approach is to call or email the admissions office of colleges and post-high school programs and ask direct questions: "Do you want four years of math on a high school transcript? Or are three years acceptable if pre-calculus is completed?" And if you feel that the person you spoke to or emailed you did not seem to know for sure, try to find another person who might actually know the answer.

(You can ask for the link to the page on the site that gives this information. Then print out the page and put it in your college application material. Information or a link may change but you will have a hard copy of the information you relied on.)

Besides the information on entry requirements for colleges and post-high school programs, there is another area of research that you should consider starting as early as the summer before 9th grade.

What are you going to be when you grow up?

This is actually a trick question. There is no way you can know this now. But you can start talking to people in different careers or vocations that may interest you. Or you can even talk to people in many different fields just to find out WHAT THEY DO.

Particularly if you have a passion at this point, you can explore possible work paths connected to that passion.

Talk to people about different vocations and career paths.

While you can do research online and in the library about possible vocations and careers, talking to a working architect, for example, can provide valuable knowledge. And you can ask questions!

There is actually an easy step-by-step process to talking to people about their careers – and usually people love talking about themselves. In the exercises at the end of this chapter, we will follow the steps for talking to an architect about this career path. The same step-by-step process can be used to talk to anyone in any career or vocational path, so be sure to do the exercises at the end of the chapter.

And, of course, the more research you have done before 9th grade on possible career paths, the better prepared you are to choose your elective schedule in 9th grade and beyond. If you have some clear ideas on your passion and possible career paths, you can choose electives to support these.

ADVANCED PLACEMENT COURSES IN HIGH SCHOOL

This topic is such a thorny path for many high school students that we are going to spend time considering this decision.

What is the big deal with AP courses?

AP courses: To take or not to take – that is the question.

First, it is important to realize that this is a BIG discussion topic for students who plan to apply to top colleges. This is because the number of AP courses offered at your high school that you took is often an important consideration for college admission officers.

Now there are actually some lucky students who attend academically challenging high schools that offer NO Advance Placement courses. These schools simply notify the colleges that the high school's policy is to offer no AP courses.

For the rest of you – you are stuck in the conundrum of Advance Placement hell.

As one college counselor at a prominent Los Angeles private high school said, there are three things college admissions people at top colleges look for on a student's high school transcript:

1) courses taken

2) grades gotten

3) courses the student could have taken based on the profile of his/her high school (In other words, how many of the high school's offered AP and honors courses you actually took.)

Advance Placement courses are considered college-level courses.

You take these Advance Placement courses as part of your high school curriculum. Then at the end of each high school year you take national AP exams in whatever AP course or courses you took that school year.

Depending on what score you get as well as the AP score requirements of the college you eventually attend, your college may give you college credit for these courses. (This is how some ambitious high school students enter college with several college credits.) For computing your high school GPA – an A in an AP course is a 5.0 rather than a 4.0 if your school uses 4.0 for an A.

On the other side of the coin, the AP courses are taught to the AP exam, which means that the teacher is compelled to keep pace with the national test curriculum. This is usually a very heavy workload. And, if you fall behind in the course, you could end up doing poorly in the course as well as the exam because there is rarely time in class to accommodate students who cannot keep up with the pace. In this scenario your high school GPA might suffer (unless you are lucky enough to have an outside tutor in that subject).

Carefully consider whether AP courses are right for your path – it is not an easy decision.

Imagine that you have taken no AP classes and have a 3.8 GPA. Yet the school offers several AP classes, which are listed in the school profile accompanying the required recommendation from your high school's college counselor. Looking at your transcript and the school's profile, a college admissions officer may have serious concerns that you were not willing to push yourself in any area. This perceived lack of effort could prevent you from getting into a top college.

The parents of a senior at a superior public high school were enraged to discover that their son – according to his college counselor – could not get into a top college as he had not taken any AP classes, something they had never been told before. While this may be a somewhat strong statement from the high school's college counselor, do think about AP courses while there is still time to take AP courses.

An admissions-involved officer at an Ivy League school put it this way: It's a question of whether to take five APs in a single school year and get all Bs or take some of these five as regular courses and get As in those. Your GPA could actually end up the same regardless of which path you choose (because of the extra point given AP class grades). And the officer did add that you do NOT need to take all the honors courses offered by your high school to get into a top college.

Strategically, it may make sense to take AP courses in subject areas in which you are strong and NOT take AP courses in subject areas that are not your strength.

Consider how you plan to present yourself in college applications.

Let's take, for an example, how you plan to present yourself on college applications. My older daughter came to me after a couple of days in AP U.S. History her junior year of high school and said, "Due to the required workload, I can either take AP U.S. History and not work on my film producing projects. Or I can switch to regular U.S. History and work on my film producing projects."

I knew her goal – to attend undergraduate film school – and her plan to present her film producing projects on college applications. Therefore, I agreed with her that she should drop AP U.S. History and instead work on her film projects. (And she did take AP English her senior year.)

Work with your parents, advisors or mentors to consider what is best for you:

First, check the AP courses offered in your high school for the four years.

Second, consider your academic strengths.

Third, evaluate the type of colleges or other post-high school programs to which you might be interested in applying and the importance of AP courses in the admissions process of those colleges and programs.

Fourth, think about how much time you will have for heavy AP course loads combined with the rest of your high school life.

THE FUN PART OF HIGH SCHOOL – EXTRACURRICULAR ACTIVITIES

And I do mean fun. While it is important to do extracurricular activities if you want to get into a top college, you should do activities that you enjoy and not ones that you only choose because you think some college admissions officer is going to be impressed.

Yes, there is more to high school life than schoolwork.

To what do you want to devote your extracurricular time?

We are talking about your elective activities both at school and outside school.

Does this look like an easy question – whatever you enjoy? Yet it can become a trick question. Because, of course, there are many things you might enjoy. That is why we need a few ground rules of what we are talking about:

What about extracurricular activities in connection with college applications?

Do **not** undertake so much that your grades suffer. Colleges want to see good grades AND additional activities, **which can include part-time jobs**.

Do **not** change activities as frequently as you change your socks. Colleges do want to see some consistency over your years of high school. Trying out a different school club each year (math club, government club, etc.) is probably not as good as sticking to one school club for the four years (and making a contribution to the success of that club).

- Do **not** participate in the activity marathon in which you compete with your classmates to see who can compile the longest list of extracurricular activities. The high school years are a time for you to pursue possible passions. To realistically evaluate the trying on of a possible passion, you must go deeper rather than wider in your overall activities.

- Do choose with your heart and soul. That is, truly select activities that both interest you and to which you can contribute in a meaningful way (not just by showing up and sleeping through a guest speaker).

Agree that extracurricular activities are NOT a competitive sport.

Extracurricular activities are about exploring possible passions for yourself, learning new things, and creating a brand for yourself. What do I mean by creating a brand? I mean that, within the few seconds that someone looks at your resume, that person should be able to get an overall cohesive picture of the person you are and hope to be (in the way that television ads in a few seconds present a product). Doing extracurricular activities that truly interest you can help make sure that this picture is an authentic one.

Pothole alert: One way in which I believe high school students shortchange their college applications – and themselves – is by only undertaking activities within the confines or sponsorship of their own high school.

Let me clarify this:

Imagine two high school students – Beth and Jane. By her senior year Beth is class president (as are thousands of other seniors across the country), plays the trombone in the marching band, is editor of the yearbook, and has repaired low-income houses in her community through a project organized by the social action club at her school.

On the other hand, Jane has taken college courses in her field of passionate interest at her community college and also online, fenced competitively at a fencing center miles from her home and participated in national fencing competitions, and on her own initiative performed monthly piano recitals at a neighborhood senior citizens center.

Which of the two high school students – given everything equal (standardized test scores, grades, essays, etc.) – might be more likely to be admitted to a top college? The student who was a leader in her own school with activities offered at the school or the student who went out into the world and created opportunities for herself?

One good way to find groups outside your high school is Meetup.com – a site on which you can search for groups by topic in your local area. And you can even start your own group!

Social media tip: *If you are interested in a writing career, there are numerous opportunities to write guest blog posts. Sites that have guest bloggers often post submission requirements. Or if there is a blog for which you really want to write a guest post, contact the blog owner and offer an original post on a specific topic relevant to the blog's overall subject matter.*

How important is doing community service for your college application resume?

Current wisdom does say that it is important to have community service on college applications. In my opinion, even when doing community service, it is more impressive to go outside the easy path – your whole camp or high school volunteers for a week to paint low-income houses – and do or develop a community service project on your own.

Community service can be a testing ground for possible careers.

Give careful consideration to your community service projects rather than just doing anything to fulfill the requirements of your school or a future college application. Often community service can be a good place to try out your future path.

Thinking about being a vet? What about volunteering in an animal shelter? Or thinking about becoming a landscape gardener? What about volunteering for a community beautification project planting trees and flowers in a blighted neighborhood?

Yes, but which activities are best for getting into top colleges?

Which colleges? Which years? Activities combined with what else you have done? Which admission officer or admission officers will read/review your application?

There is only one sure thing:

It is impossible to predict which activities would be the best.

There is no way to know what general types of activities which colleges in any which years will be looking for on applications. For example, some years a particular college band may need trombone players, some years flute players. Some colleges may be more impressed by volunteer work helping the needy, others by entrepreneurial projects that made you money. And the same schools can change their priorities from year to year.

Then what is a teen to do?

One thing a teen can do is NOT do what every other teen in America is doing. My number one example of this? Spending the summer before 12th grade as a camp counselor – either day camp or overnight camp. If you really, really want to be a camp counselor where you were once a camper, then wait until the summer AFTER you graduate high school. The summer BEFORE 12th grade do something interesting and different from all your college admission competition.

Think outside the box regarding extracurricular activities.

Go on the Internet or to a public library or bookstore and look for ideas on things you can do while in high school. Think beyond the activities offered by your school, scout troop or whatever. Think global projects that can be done online, working with a legal aid society in your town, or starting a music program at the senior citizen center down the block.

One such outside the box possibility is Outward Bound training (http://www.outwardbound.org/), which is especially strong in certain areas such as teamwork – an ability considered very important in many career tracks. Imagine, in an interview, how you could demonstrate your ability to work with others by describing your Outward Bound team experience.

And if you need to do extracurricular activities that do not cost your family any money? Or you need to work to make money for your family?

If you think outside the box, you will probably be able to find free activities as well as jobs that make you stand out from the competition.

For example, let's say you work at Starbucks to make money for your family. Maybe you could ask your supervisor if you could organize a weekly read-to-tots event at the store where you work. And for half an hour each week you read to a group of two-year-olds while their caregivers sit in another area of the store and purchase Starbucks beverage and food items.

Your supervisor will probably think you are terrific (this activity supports the Starbucks brand as a home away from home) and write a glowing recommendation for you. Plus you yourself will have something meaningful to add to your college application resume – a community service project that you started and did all by yourself.

What about the question of well-rounded or specialist?

Do colleges want well-rounded students or specialists?

There are many opinions on both sides of the question, and surely the answer is not the same for all colleges. Basically the assumption is that colleges want a well-rounded freshman class – each individual student with his or her particular interests adds to an overall mix of diverse students. In other words, colleges are looking for what some call "well-lopsided" students – students whose passions can contribute to a dynamic college campus life.

In many cases, top grades and top standardized test scores are not enough. You have to show something else – something else that defines who you are and makes you stand out from all the others.

A University of Southern California admissions officer told this story: He interviewed a young man who did not seem to have anything special going for him. At the end of the interview the young man mentioned that he painted landscapes, something he had not thought to include on his resume. The admissions officer asked if the student had any paintings with him. Indeed, the student did – in his car. He showed these to the admissions officer, and those paintings got the young man admitted to USC.

Are there ways to stand out in following your passion?

Yes, there are. And thanks to the Internet there are more and more opportunities to get your work/talent out there.

Apply to competitions/contests in areas of your passion.

For example, if writing or drawing or poster design or model building is your passion and there is a local or national competition in that field for which you are eligible, enter the competition. Doing well in such a competition is a great way to demonstrate your passion as well as have your talent validated by an outside source.

Keep work in a portfolio or online portfolio for easy show-and-tell.

Social media tip: The social media site http://pinterest.com offers a platform that could be excellent for showcasing your work. On Pinterest you could have different "boards" (collages) for different projects, and each "board" is made up of several "pins" (a pin is an image with accompanying description and, if appropriate, a link).

What if you are not a leader?

If colleges or the workforce had all leaders, who would be the followers who work together with the leaders to get things done?

Some people are leaders and some are not.

What defines a leader? Someone who is the president of the high school glee club? Or president of the high school investor club? Both these students may be president although they may not do any actual leading in the sense of forging ahead into new areas or activities.

On the other hand, a student who is a rank-and-file member of a high school community service club may develop an innovative reading program for children in a homeless shelter.

Instead of worrying, say, about getting elected president of your high school stamp club, look around for meaningful projects in the fields of passion you are exploring. The possibilities are endless: designing scenery for a community theater production (art or design passion), implementing an after-school reading program at an elementary school (teaching passion), working with a community group to fix-up low-income housing (carpentry or architecture passion).

Social media tip: *You can share these projects online to encourage others to find ways to experiment with their possible passions. And the exchange of information can be beneficial to everyone.*

You can be president of any club you start yourself.

What is the big deal about making choices?

The Internet has done many wonderful things. Stretching a 24-hour day into more hours is not one of those things.

Make good choices in a time-bound world.

Yes, you have to keep up your grades while having some time

off for fun and yet still getting nightly those at least eight hours of sleep everyone is always harping a growing teen needs plus monthly visits to your grandparents, watering the lawn, taking out the trash, and … everything else.

I hear you. This is exactly why you have to make choices. And why the best time to start planning is the summer before 9th grade before your four-year class schedule is set in stone. By planning now you actually make it easier for yourself later.

Is there anything else you should take into account when planning for extracurricular activities?

Do you have a favorite method of keeping track of things: online calendars, personal diaries, large calendar hung on your bedroom door? Whatever it is, take a good look at your average school-year week. What time does your school get out? Will you need time in later years of high school to work part-time? If there is no public transportation available, how much chauffeuring is reasonable to ask your parents or others to do for you?

Figure out your time constraints.

In other words, first figure out as realistically as you can what your constraints are in terms of school work, family responsibilities, part-time job. Then consider what you **tentatively** might like to do in terms of passion and extracurricular activities during your four years of high school and, most importantly, during the three summers between 9th and 12th grades.

Write down your tentative activity ideas with an estimate of how much time each activity/job will take. Now you have something to show as a starting point when you talk with adults who can help you plan. Of course, over your high school years your tentative ideas will change as you outgrow some activities and discover new ones. The point for now is to do tentative planning so you have a starting point.

Before you sit down with adults to talk about possible activities, show those adults the following note:

NOTE FOR PARENTS, ADVISORS AND MENTORS:

Most entering 9th graders (or graduating high school seniors) do not instinctively know how to write a request for an adult to meet with them for what is called an informational meeting. Nor do these students have practice calling up an adult to ask for a 10-minute meeting on, say, what marine biologists do.

Thus these high school years are a golden opportunity for adults to forge a bond with teens by working with them on life skills. These are skills that can be used throughout life, so learning these skills earlier rather than later makes good sense. (You may be excellent at giving your teen music lessons, sports lessons, or language lessons, yet not realize that you also have a responsibility to give teens life lessons. Unfortunately these skills are not taught in most high schools.)

For example, if your teen asks you to help prepare for a phone conversation with an insurance actuary to learn what career options there are in this field, ROLE PLAY the conversation. And hit your teen with fast balls as well as slow balls in this role playing. Practicing with teens how to handle hostile conversations may be one of the best gifts you can give them.

High school students need to learn that they may call someone to ask for a brief meeting – and get an earful of anger. These students need to take a deep breath and realize the anger is NOT about them. The person called may have been very busy at the moment and thus resentful of **any** interruption. And if the student had called at a different time, the response could have been cordial. (This is one reason an email may be a better first approach than a phone call.)

Actively participate with your high school students in this high-school-as-preparation-for-adult-life experience. It is better to have a young person strike out on an interview question you threw at him/her instead of when it really counts – during an interview for the internship or job or college that he/she truly wants.

What about high schools' college counselors?

Most public high schools have a serious shortage of college counselors. Private schools usually have a better ratio, yet the counselors are still attuned to the students who fit the usual parameters – high grades or low grades or whatever labels are used. In addition, although some schools start college advising in the spring of 11th grade and some enlightened schools start earlier, many schools do not start advising until fall of 12th grade. And, frankly, this is too late for good college admissions planning.

Understand what high schools' college counselors can do.

Unfortunately, there is something else to consider about high school college counselors. They are not all created equally with the same amount of knowledge and experience, and they may have their own agendas for whatever reasons.

Here is an example of a possible personal agenda: A counselor may want to demonstrate how successful he/she is in helping students get into the colleges to which they apply. To ensure a better acceptance rate, the counselor may steer students to apply to less academically oriented schools.

Therefore, you cannot take everything one specific college counselor says as the absolute non-refutable truth.

What these counselors can usually give you is the general overall information that is good for everyone: when to take the standardized tests, when to ask for your high school recommendations, etc.

What these counselors usually do **not** have time for is to know each and every student well enough to figure out the best places for each individual student to apply.

And what these counselors in most cases definitely do not have time for is to check up on whether each student is meeting the test-taking and application deadlines.

Become your own best source of information.

You and your parents, advisors or mentors have to be on top of what is out there in the way of colleges and other post-high school programs that may be good for you. And while you will not need to know all this until the end of 11th grade or the beginning of 12th , it is a good idea in 9th grade to start keeping an eye on what is out there.

How do you keep track of all this information you are going to collect?

You are going to start an organization system.

One possibility is getting a three-ring binder, a three-hole punch, and alphabet tabs (or make your own tabs). Then start collecting information you find about different colleges or post-high school programs of interest. This might be material you pick up at a college or job fair. Or magazine articles you save. Or brochures that come in the mail. Or articles you print off the Internet.

Punch this material down (or, if awkward sizes, first attach to a sheet of paper and then punch down). Then file this material behind tabs of the college name or the kind of program offered, such as landscaping.

Be sure to label the name of the newspaper/magazine from which you took the article and the date of the publication.

Newspapers and magazines have their own biases while things at a college can change. When it comes time to make your list of where you plan to apply, you will want to know how current and reliable your saved information is. And you can check this stored information against current information available on the Internet, etc.

Choose an organizational system that works for you.

Maybe you would rather set up a computer tracking system with notes about the various programs that interest you. You will input the most important info from material you read. Again, though, date the notes and where the information is from.

Anything else of which you should keep track?

Also keep notes on which colleges the older students from your school attend. That way, for example, if you decide that American University is your top choice and you know that Susan, two years older, attends American, you have someone from your high school to contact for information.

What is more, Susan is an ideal person to talk to because she comes from the same education system as you. If, for example, you ask her how well-prepared she was for college work and you discuss specific teachers you both had, you will have a better picture than if you ask another student at American University who attended a different education system.

Social media tip: *There are alumni groups on various social media sites. Sometimes you must be an actual alum to participate in a specific group. If there is not this requirement, consider joining such groups for the colleges that interest you. While I would **not** recommend you ask for help getting into the particular school, you can ask appropriate questions about the specific college experience.*

And what about those adults to whom you have access?

Most high school students do not pay attention to what their parents' friends and their friends' parents do. Yet when it comes time, for example, to look for an internship in a specific field, such as investment banking, it sure would be nice to remember that Jeffrey's mother is an investment banker at a major investment firm in your hometown.

Track the careers and colleges attended of the adults you know.

And when it comes time to see if you can get a college application recommendation from someone who went to the college to which you are applying, say the University of Chicago, it would be great to remember that Max's father attended this university and, in fact, is active in the alumni association.

INTRODUCTION TO INTERNSHIPS

What are we talking about here?

We are not talking about what doctors do after they finish medical school. We are talking about the opportunity to try on a possible career track, usually as an unpaid worker.

Have at least one internship experience while in high school.

Because of the importance of internships during college in order to prepare for life after college, I go into much more depth about internships in the second book in this series – HOW TO SUCCEED IN COLLEGE AND PREP FOR BEYOND COLLEGE.

For now let's look at the place of internships in the application process for college or other post-high school programs.

What can an internship do for you?

Imagine that Joseph is a junior at an excellent public high school. He has done extremely well on the standardized tests and has a high grade point average. His goal is to apply to a top undergraduate business school next year because he has always been interested in business.

Yet nothing in Joseph's resume supports his interest in business. Sure, he has done a lot of activities in school – sports, drama club, student council – and in the summers he has attended a debate camp and been a day camp counselor. SHOW ME THE BUSINESS INTEREST.

Joseph will be competing against huge numbers of other students with high standardized test scores and grades who have interned at an investment firm, started their own Internet business, and/or taken business courses at a nearby community college or online. If you were an admissions officer of the elite business school to which he is applying, would you choose Joseph based on his written statement that he is interested in business over another applicant who has demonstrated a passion for business by her actions (perhaps by starting her own online t-shirt business)?

When should you do an internship or internships?

Even if up until the end of 11th grade you have not demonstrated your professed passion, the summer before 12th grade gives you one last chance to do so. And an internship in the field of your interest can be a powerful statement on your college or post-high school program application. (Of course, internships in an earlier summer or during the school year add icing to the cake.)

The summer before 12th grade is one last chance to intern.

And, yes, many students have to work full-time in the summer to earn money for college. Yet with some judicious juggling of time you can hold down a full-time job in the summer and still have a part-time internship. In fact, this can demonstrate to a college admissions officer real commitment on your part if you work fulltime and still do a part-time internship.

Work fulltime and intern during summer vacations.

Want an example of how to do this? If you work at the Gap and take two night shifts and/or weekend days, you can squeeze in the time for a two-days-a-week internship at an interior design firm. Or work a regular Monday through Friday 9-5 job and intern two evenings a week at a legal aid society open evenings. (And, remember, you do not have any homework during summer vacations unless you are taking summer school.)

Internships are not indentured servant status.

Internships do NOT have to be five days a week. And they do NOT have to be for the entire summer. You are only looking for a taste of this particular experience.

A FINAL WORD ABOUT WORDS

What is the big deal about learning new words?

Learn a new word every day. Make it a part of your daily schedule – maybe when you are brushing your teeth or waiting for your computer to boot up. This is a habit you can carry through to adult life. It is not only good for improving your standardized test scores, it is good for writing business memos or reading textbooks or The Wall Street Journal.

Expand your vocabulary.

Your parents, advisors or mentors can help by using big words and giving you the meaning of these words. From the time my daughters were little, I always used big words with them, gave the definition of the word, and followed with this mantra: "Remember this word. It will be on the SATs."

There is another way to learn new words – READ BOOKS! Turn off the Internet and read a book that is **not** assigned for school. (Or read an ebook online or on an ereader.) You will increase both your vocabulary (use a dictionary or online dictionary for words you do not know) and your reading ability.

Pothole alert: If you are writing essays for college applications, do NOT stuff all those new BIG words into the essays. When you write essays you want to follow the creative writing rule NOT to use little-known words that can interfere with the essay reader's concentration because the meaning of a word must be puzzled out. You want to use words that a reader can quickly absorb as he/she reads your well-written essay.

Do the following exercises before you read the next chapter.

EXERCISES

(There is no teacher or parent standing over you demanding that you do all this work. These exercises are like most other things in life – you get what you pay for. If you do the exercises, you should get a benefit. It you do not do these, you have passed up an opportunity to improve your skills.)

Exercise A:

1) Choose one career path that may interest you. Ask your teachers and others which people they know who have this career path. As an example, at this point you may be interested in architecture. You would ask for names and contact information for local architects. If your teachers and others do not know any such people, you can use search functions on sites such as LinkedIn to look for such people.

2) Now that you have the name and contact info of at least one local architect, call or email her. If calling, practice your call first. (And when you call, do not launch into a long speech. Ask if this is a good time to speak and, if not, ask when would be a better time to call.) If

emailing (which can prevent a possibly awkward phone situation), make sure you run spell check and then read the text aloud to ensure no words have been added or left out. Explain that you are considering a career in architecture and ask whether she would have time to speak to you on the phone or meet you for 15 minutes to answer some questions about the career. (If someone recommended you contact this architect and the person gave you permission to use his/her name, do so.)

3) Presumably you have found someone who will talk to you. If meeting in person, be sure to practice beforehand all the tips in Chapter II, including good posture, strong handshake, leaving "like" and "you know" and your gum outside the office door. If talking on the phone, practice beforehand speaking slowly and enunciating and not dropping your voice at the end of sentences.

4) Be prepared with questions to ask, such as: Would you recommend a career in architecture for young people now? (Perhaps the occupation has become oversaturated and there are too many architects for the available jobs.) What courses in high school did you take that helped prepare you for this career? What activities can I do outside high school to improve my success in this possible career path?

5) Have the **brief** conversation with the architect. (Do not go over the 10 or 15 minutes you have promised unless the person offers for you to have more time.) **Take notes while you talk/meet with her.** Then type up your notes and place them in your ring binder or other organizational system.

6) Send a handwritten note to the architect thanking her for her time. Yes, handwritten and not emailed. Handwritten notes make a big impression.

7) If you had a good rapport with the architect and she offered for you to keep in touch, do so even if you are not sure you will ultimately apply to an architectural program. If you take a high school course she recommended or do an outside project she recommended, let her know you followed through on her advice. Who knows, she could be an internship or recommendation source

for you in the future – and people like to know that their advice has been followed.

8)   If you cannot find any such people in your hometown, expand your search to people outside your town. In this case you would be asking for a phone conversation or even a brief email exchange to ask your questions. (This is where searching on a professional social media site such as LinkedIn can be very helpful.)

Exercise B:

1)   Pick a college you have heard of that may be of interest to you at this time. Research information on the Internet about the college (the college's website, the college's social media activities such as a Facebook Page, and online articles that mention the school).

2)   Study what the college says it is looking for in prospective students.

3)   Consult the high school course curriculum you have tentatively mapped out. Do you think the courses you plan to take fulfill the expectations of this college? (Note: For this exercise do NOT choose a college with easy admission requirements. Choose one with more stringent admission requirements in order to expand your future options.)

4)   Record the notes on what you have learned. Put the notes into your   ring   binder   or   into   your   online   records.

Exercise C:

1)   Write a practice essay on why at this early stage in your high school career you might want to be, say, a sports reporter. Practice all the effective writing techniques you are learning in your English classes to make the essay as vivid as possible. Use words (but not BIG words) that create pictures in the reader's mind to provide a clear understanding of why this particular career may appeal to you – such as *how* it builds on your strengths, minimizes your weaknesses,

appeals to your love of sports, etc. Notice the word *how*. Do **not**, for example, simply say the career builds on your strengths and name the strengths. Demonstrate *how* the career builds on your strengths.

2)   Show the essay to someone and ask if the essay clearly conveys your interest in becoming a sports reporter. Does the person reading your essay have any relevant questions for you about this possible career path that are not answered in the essay?

3)   Rewrite your essay based on the above feedback.

4)   Put the rewritten essay in your ring binder (or your college admission folder on your computer) for reference when you write essays for your college applications. (It is to be hoped that the essays you write in 12th grade for college applications will be stronger writing samples than the ones you write earlier in your high school career. The goal is to steadily improve your writing skills during high school. The **ideas** of the earlier essays are what you are saving for future reference.)

CHAPTER IV: APPLYING TO COLLEGE

If you are just starting to read this book now while you are already a junior in high school, go back and read the previous chapters.

I am not suggesting you read the previous chapters so you can feel badly about what you have not done. I am suggesting you read these chapters for what ideas can be utilized now to help you with this process and with learning important life skills. (And for those of you who read the previous chapters a long time ago, a little review might be a good idea.)

Here comes the big announcement:

THE COLLEGE YOU GET INTO AND ATTEND DOES NOT DEFINE WHO YOU ARE FOREVER AND EVER.

This is not a contest that, if you do not win (that is, get into the college of your first choice), it is downhill from here. On the contrary, the college that you desperately wanted to attend may have ended up being wrong for you. And the college you actually attend may turn out to be terrific for your interests and abilities.

And what is more, for many career paths the college attended is not that important. Or if it is, by the second job the gap can be closed.

Imagine Fred, who gets a B.A. from an Ivy but never learns life skills and so does not make the most out of the opportunity his degree might afford him. Then there is Susan, who gets a B.A. from a little-known college in the Midwest yet uses life skills to propel herself onto a winning career path.

Does what college you attend have an impact on further steps on your path in life?

All things being equal, it is probably true that doing well at a good undergraduate school will help you get into a good graduate school or help you get a good first job.

All things are NOT equal.

Initiative, commitment, research, networking (offline and online), luck and many other elements figure into a future career path. All of these elements are things that you can work on and influence.

And things are radically different now than they were for your parents' generation or grandparents' generation.

Here is my personal favorite story: In the summer of 1965 before my senior year of high school I had an admission interview at the University of Pennsylvania. The interviewer (who had not seen my grades or SAT scores) said: "You are a girl from the Midwest. You will never get in." (Not one but two strikes against me.) I did not protest to him and I not apply – and 25 years later I graduated from Penn's Wharton School with an M.B.A.

During those 25 years, the attitude of prominent Eastern schools towards non-Easterns and towards females changed drastically. Diversity of geographical region and ethnic background and gender (many formerly single-sex colleges turned co-ed) became the norm for Eastern colleges.

Make good things happen for yourself.

No matter where you end up going to college, it is not the end of the world. In fact, it is the beginning.

What about strategizing for getting into the best school for you?

First, let's be clear we are on the same page. The definition of best school for you includes:

- ranking compared to other colleges (and note what the rankings are based on in the various places where these rankings occur – for example, how much do the attributes such as average class size matter to you)
- location that appeals to you (rural, urban, small city, large city)

- size of school (this is a tricky area) – average class size may be a better indicator than school size; you can attend a huge university with a vast array of courses, athletics and activities yet find your niche of friends/activities and be oblivious to the thousands of other students around you; do some research into how the size of the school translates into opportunities for less popular majors, undergraduate research opportunities, etc.
- majors offered
- only undergraduates on campus or both undergraduates and graduate students on the same campus

- campus life
- competitive sports teams (if you are eyeing a run for the Olympics in a particular sport this is probably quite important; on the other hand, if you are injured freshman year and can no longer participate in the sport, will you still want to be at that college)
- and numerous other things that are important to you, including cost of attending the college, distance from home, ease of getting there (some colleges are truly out in the boonies), and, if you want to do a year abroad, what are the school's opportunities and requirements for doing this

Spend time considering what things are important to you.

To which colleges should you apply?

Make a list of colleges you have heard about or someone has told you about that sound as if they might appeal to you. You can ask for help from all kinds of people to create this preliminary list.

For example, maybe you list only colleges in your home state. Or only colleges that have Big 10 football teams. Whatever. At this point you do not need to limit yourself.

Now the work begins. You have to research this list.

If you need help with coming up with a preliminary list:

Some high schools have database programs that allow you to search by desired major, location, academic rigor, etc. Or the high school libraries have books available for researching colleges. You can go to a bookstore or public library for books on colleges.

And of course there is the Internet. In fact, the College Board's website www.collegeboard.org has a college search engine that enables you to search by various criteria.

Set up an organizational system for tracking college info.

What do you do next?

More research.

You can research the individual colleges by checking out their websites and other available information on the Internet. Remember the information on colleges that you have been collecting if you read the earlier chapters of this book?

First get as much information as you can. And, yes, it is fair to ask parents, advisors or mentors to help with this research if you are busy interning, doing community service, going to school, playing sports, working at a paying job.

Now is the time to get up close-and-personal with current students or very recent graduates of the schools that interest you. Remember that even someone who graduated only five years ago from a particular college may not know what the school is like now.

Things can change a great deal in five years, and not just new dorms and new buildings but new programs and new student polices and new student academic requirements. And you can always ask someone who graduated from a particular school a long time ago if he/she can introduce you to a current student or recent graduate of that school.

Social media tip: Here is where social media can be particularly useful in finding and connecting with current and recent graduates of a school. I recommend, though, that you discuss specifics either offline or in personal emails rather than via social media sites.

What about the range of grades and standardized test scores listed for the typical accepted student at a particular college?

Yes, you should look at these ranges BUT, if you know that you will have a lot going for you at the time you apply, do **not** accept as written-in-stone what your high school's college counselor says about your applying to a particular school.

If you think you have a chance at a particular college.

Let's say your grades and standardized test scores are pretty close to the ballpark of the school's ranges AND you will have a recommendation from an alum with whom you interned AND you have done an incredible community service project, AND etc. In this case you may be a much better candidate than a student with grades and standardized test scores smack in the middle of the school's range but without the extras that you have.

If you have these three things going for you:

a) realistic about your chances given your grades and standardized test scores compared to the specific college's range for these indicators

b) built a strong resume for that college

c) confident your essays will be well-written

You should consider applying to that college regardless of what your high school's guidance counselor says.

This whole process of deciding which colleges to apply to is similar to figuring out strategy for any competitive sport. Do you bat the ball to center field or try for a home run? Do you hit the tennis ball just over the net or smash it almost out of bounds? In competitive sports as in college applications, you make the best decisions based on the information you have.

How do you keep track of everything?

Decide what is best for your personality for tracking standardized test registration dates, application deadlines, requests for recommendation, and all the seemingly endless details that go into applying for college.

A simple system may be a wall calendar with all dates on it – perhaps using different color pens for different stages. A note written in red may represent 5 days before something is due, a note in green means 3 days, a note in black means this is the last day, period.

Then you may have a separate file folder for each of the different requirements: one for standardized tests, one for each college, one for all recommendations so they can be tracked together, etc.

Here is the system my sister recommends based on her two sons applying to college:

Make a physical matrix that lists the schools you are applying to, with due dates across the top as well as the dates the high school requires you to turn in the needed information. Post the matrix where you can see it every day. It is not enough to have it on the computer because that requires you to open up the calendar page and look at it. Posted on your wall is much more jarring. That way it is always staring you in the face. Even if you think you can remember, this helps.

Get a college application buddy.

If organization is not your strong suit, consider finding a college application buddy who is good at organizing. In exchange for having him/her keep you organized, you offer to do something for him/her at which you are good.

(Even if you do not have attention-concentration concerns, you may find helpful the organization techniques in the book "ADD-Friendly Ways to Organize Your Life" by Judith Kolberg & Kathleen Nadeau, Ph.D. In this stressful time of college applications, every piece of advice may help.)

THOSE ALL IMPORTANT ESSAYS

What if it is the end of junior year or the beginning of senior year of high school – is it too late to improve your attractiveness to colleges?

At this time in your high school career some things are beyond your control to change. You cannot change that chemistry grade you got in 10th grade. (Yes, I know the teacher hated you; yet do you really want to write your college application essay about this?) And if it is the fall of senior year – you cannot change that you have had no involvement in what you will state on your college applications as your passion.

Is there something you can control?

Your ESSAYS.

You can take this part of the application process quite seriously and write really good essays.

Go the extra mile to write really good essays.

Here is a true story about someone who was not accepted into a top business school MBA program. He called the school and asked why he had not been accepted. The answer: his essay was weak. At that time, 10 essays were read in a row and then the reader started over again. If the reader could not remember from an essay's first paragraph what the essay was about, the essay was deemed weak.

This is how important an essay can be in the application process. **And it is the one thing that you can truly control.**

What topic should you choose to write on for your main essay?

An important part of the essay writing is the first step – choosing the topic for the main essay. While many college applications ask somewhat specific questions, the actual topics may provide choices for you.

Carefully consider what to write.

Carefully consider your options – brainstorm with others to see which ideas might come across the best to a reader who does not know you personally.

Do not automatically answer the question without trying to think outside the box – try not to write the same thing that the other applicants will write (for example, how meaningful it was to be senior class president, about making the winning touchdown, etc.).

What if an application asks for several essays?

A college application requiring several essays – perhaps one long and three shorter ones – is an OVERALL PACKAGE. All the essays should connect to one overall story – and I do not mean a fictional story. In other words, strategize how the long and short essays go together to create a cohesive and positive (and truthful!) picture of who you are. And also consider which segment of your experiences deserves the long essay spotlight.

Let me explain:

You probably have several interesting attributes you want to get across to an admissions committee. You may, for example, spend a considerable amount of time writing the main essay about your visit to Russia three summers ago as an example of a major experience that changed your life.

Suddenly you realize that this particular piece of information would be better suited for one of the shorter essays in the same application (the one about what you like to do for fun outside of school) while your experience working with mentally disabled children at a homeless shelter would be better suited to the main essay.

Be flexible about changing around your essays.

In the above example, if you are applying to a college with the stated major of becoming a special education teacher, it makes more sense to write your main essay on the specific example of your work in this field. Thus the major essay supports this stated goal while one of the shorter essays portrays you as someone who likes to travel.

How do you choose whether to do question A or B for your main essay when you are given two choices?

The goal is **not** to show off how you can answer a challenging question. The goal is to write the best essay you can that presents your uniqueness to the college. And, of course, that uniqueness can be different for different colleges to which you apply.

Give as much thought to what you will write about as you do to the actual writing. It is worth the effort!

Write only to the length indicated for each essay.

You will NOT get extra points for writing longer essays. In fact, you may get demerits for not following instructions.

If you are over the word count, work on editing your essay down to the correct length. In the process you may be making the essay more effective.

Only include material that belongs in the essay.

On the other hand, if your essay is considerably shorter than the indicated word count, do NOT add adjectives and adverbs to get up to the correct count. Expand the essay with additional material that belongs in that essay and adds to the overall essay's theme.

Pothole alert: Do NOT include a laundry list of activities in a long essay. Instead focus on one particular activity and portray this in a compelling (and truthful!) manner. Laundry lists are not interesting – and much of the information is often included elsewhere on a college application.

What makes a good essay?

Yes, evaluating an essay can be subjective. Yet there are a few points that, if mastered, can make a big difference on the effectiveness of any essay.

Make the first paragraph memorable.

Now I do not mean something wild that has nothing to do with the rest of the essay. The first paragraph MUST be consistent with the overall essay.

What I mean is this – most of us have a tendency to warm up to our subject in the first paragraph of an essay. Then it is not until the second paragraph that we get to the specific nitty gritty of what we are saying.

Here is an easy solution to this tendency:

Write that warm-up paragraph. Then, in the rewriting stage, toss it out and strengthen the original second paragraph into a strong first paragraph.

And make sure that new first paragraph sticks in the reader's mind.

Be specific – paint compelling word pictures.

Many of us talk and write in generalities. Talking about peace does not register a concept as vividly as does talking about a village in Africa with only two weeks free of gunfire exchanges in the last 10 years. Use specific rather than general words – the images conveyed will be stronger in the reader's mind. (Remember, by specific I do not mean BIG words.)

And you might even consider actual pictures if appropriate. My older daughter's essay for NYU's Tisch School of the Arts included a photo collage she made to showcase the main point of her essay.

Memorable does not depend on the topic of the essay.

MEMORABLE DOES **NOT** MEAN YOU HAVE TO WRITE ABOUT A WEIGHTY TOPIC SUCH AS WORLD PEACE.

Go to a bookstore or the library or online and find examples of effective college application essays. Read several essays and study the recurring patterns in effective essays.

One thing you should notice is that some essays are on everyday subjects, perhaps about a rare button collection, and yet are extremely powerful essays. Well-written essays on any topic can effectively demonstrate an applicant's creativity and his/her unique personality.

Also notice how few essays deal with global subjects such as world peace. It is hard for a 17- or 18-year-old to speak/write knowledgably about such topics. And unless the topic is brought down to a very specific problem, such as that village in Africa, the topic is so broad as to lack visual images that can resonate with the reader.

Check out the language used in the sample essays. Lofty language is not necessary – you do not have to use all those multi-syllable standardized test vocabulary words you memorized. There is a belief in creative writing that unusual words interrupt the "fictive dream" – these unusual words take a reader out of the story, at which point the reader's interest may be lost. While you want to write vivid specific descriptions, you should use everyday language to keep the reader's attention locked into your essay.

Here is an example of good descriptive writing:

The moment I learned I had made the varsity basketball team I choked on a Haagen-Dazs ice cream bar.

And here is an example of descriptive writing that does not work very well:

At the moment my evolutionarily developed brain processed the Darwinian concept that I had indeed made the varsity basketball team, I was eating a calorie-laden snack.

Write about things that are really meaningful to you.

Be willing to risk exposing your true thoughts and feelings even if these are emotional or touchy feely. You are not delivering an academic lecture in front of an audience of nuclear physicists. You are revealing your uniqueness to admission officers who want to know the real you.

Here is an example of what NOT to write:

When my grandfather died suddenly I felt very sad.

Here is a better version of this information:

Standing at my grandfather's grave during the funeral service, I realized that we would never again share a late night fudge sundae or together root for the Yankees.

Why is one well-developed idea worth more than 10 undeveloped ideas in an essay?

Let me explain this by the following example: You are writing an essay about why you want to be a doctor. You write each new paragraph about one or two different things you have down on your path to being a doctor. The more important things get lumped together with the less important things, almost as if you had just listed the items.

Now let's say the most important thing for this essay is the three months you spent training to be a paramedic and then actually being a volunteer paramedic. Instead of stating this information in the midst of other information, why not focus the entire essay on this one experience?

How do you do that?

You could, for example, start your essay with a paragraph about the first time after paramedic training someone's life depended on how well you did what you had learned. But instead of writing this rather trite-sounding information, you could write:

For one second my mind froze at the sight of blood dripping down the face of the bombing victim – someone who looked the same age as my younger sister. I gulped a big breath of air, shook my head, and said to myself, "You've been trained what to do. Now do it – and try to save her life!"

After this dramatic opening you could continue to describe the actual event, interlacing information on the training you had and how you used the training: *I twisted the bandage into a tourniquet the way we had practiced in paramedic training.*

Each paragraph would be a very specific part of the same story. In this way you slow down the telling and give the reader time to smell the flowers. And your feelings would come through clearly without using trite expressions such as "I was scared."

Keep the kitchen sink out of your essays.

And there is another saying that goes along with this concept – "less is more."

A compelling essay such as the example above will stay in the mind of a reader much longer and stronger than an episodic essay with each paragraph listing one or two things you did in preparation for considering a medical career.

Do you really have to rewrite the essay once you have written it?

Good writing is rewriting.

Once you have written the **first draft** of the essay, you still have a way to go before the essay is ready to be submitted. If you start writing the essay with enough time before the college application deadline, you will be able to put the essay away for a day or so and then return to it.

Take a break before re-reading your essay.

Without taking a break from writing an essay, you can easily lose interest, which makes it harder to do revisions.

Now after a day or two, read the essay as if this is your first time reading it. See where the words are awkward, where you have not made your point as convincingly as you thought you had. And now rewrite.

After your first revision – show your essay to someone for advice.

It always helps to get a second opinion. You may believe you have made something perfectly clear, but a reader may be confused. Listen carefully to the person's opinion without feeling the need to defend what you have written. If something is unclear in the person's feedback, politely ask for clarification.

If the advice is given orally, take notes. And repeat back to the person what you think the person said: *"You think it is unclear what I actually did on the ambulance race to the hospital."* This gives the person the opportunity to clarify the advice: *"I understood what you did. I was confused about how much time lapsed between the ambulance leaving the scene of the bombing and arriving at the hospital."*

Now go back to your essay and consider what parts of the person's advice make sense to you and what parts do not really pertain to your essay. (Another person's opinion is not always correct.)

Revise again – and do spell check each time you revise.

And, finally, read your essay aloud. You may be surprised to discover that your mind has automatically read a word correctly that when you speak the word turns out to be incorrect.

One last grammar and spelling check.

You need to make sure to the best of your ability that your essays are **free of spelling and grammar mistakes**. This means that you cannot rely only on spell check and grammar check.

Unless you are confident that you are the best speller and grammar person you know, have someone else who is good in these areas read over your final draft essays. You just might learn that you wrote *their* when you meant *there* (and even reading aloud would not have caught the mistake).

What about that almost universal essay question "why this college"?

University admission officers are smart people. Especially after reading thousands of student essays, they can clearly tell when a "why this college" essay is not specific to that school. This unspecific essay could be used for any school with only a different school's name and city plugged into the essay.

Here are two sentences from an opening paragraph of a student's "why this college" essay:

"A world-renowned university known both for its outstanding liberal arts education as well as its strong commitment to undergraduate research." This takes in a huge number of schools. *"A gorgeous campus in the heart of a vibrant city."* Not all colleges have a "gorgeous campus in the heart of a vibrant city," but many do.

These two sentences are not nearly specific enough. And, in addition, these statements are very weak for an opening paragraph.

You must be very, very specific about the "why" – and you can do this by research on the web (if you have not visited the campus) or by speaking to current students or alums of the college. And if you are not willing to do the research, do you really want to attend this college?

Do the research to write specific "why this college" essays.

How do you do this?

First, **on the school's website:** research specific programs, courses, etc., and refer to these by their specific names. (Not that you are interested in "economics classes" but that you are interested, for example, in "Economics of the Soviet Union during the Stalin Era.") If there is a particular program that interests you, do not just list the program. Instead, describe what you can envision yourself doing in connection with the program. The more research you do, the more specific information you will have.

Second, do research **on the web about the city** or nearest city. Instead of saying that the city has "great art museums," give specific museum names and what interests you at those museums. For example, if you are applying to a college in New York City and you are interested in armor, you might mention that you are interested in spending time at the "Arms and Armor" collection at the Metropolitan Museum of Art.

This does **not** mean you have previously seen the collection. And you should NOT say you have seen the collection if you have not. Nor should you say you are interested in art museums if you are not – choose another specific example that does interest you.

By citing a specific collection at a specific museum, you demonstrate that you have taken the time to find out which New York art museum has a collection of something that particularly interests you. At the same time you have also created a more interesting picture of yourself in the mind of the application reader than would have been created by the words "great art museums." You have made yourself stand out.

Of course, **if someone in your family attended the school**, you could include in your "why this college" essay what this relative has told you about the school. You could also mention what you have learned from talking to current students or other alums.

Why should you put lots of time into writing good essays?

Let me say this as clearly as possible: GOOD ENOUGH IS NOT GOOD ENOUGH.

Step up to the plate and face the competitive challenge.

Much of the advice in this book will be useful for your path in life, wherever that path may lead you.

One place your path is almost sure to go is into competitive situations where you will be vying for a job or a raise or a promotion with others. In all of these cases, you have to do much better than good enough.

And in the case of your college application essays, you will be competing with applicants who have had the benefit of private coaches and/or high school counselors who have insisted on top-notch essays. (Top-notch essays are those essays written and rewritten and rewritten until they are the absolute best they can be.)

This does **not** mean that, if you are a math whiz, you have to pretend that you are also a writing whiz. What this **does** mean is that you must work very hard to demonstrate good reasoning skills, good organizational skills, good topic sentence skills, good specific word usage skills, and all the other skills that your English teachers have or have not hammered into you all these years of high school. (These skills are, of course, in addition to good spelling, grammar, capitalization and punctuation.)

All these skills are critical for success in college. And this is one reason the essays are so important in the admission decision process – because your essays are a preview of what your skills will be in your college work. In other words, which students are the most likely to be successful at a particular college.

Another reason for the emphasis on essays is that they can help distinguish among students who all have the same grades, same standardized test scores, same activities, same everything. An entertainment industry executive – when talking about a studio cutting its ties with a famous actor – said: "It comes down to who you want to work with."

The same can also be said of accepting students to a particular college – it may come down to which students the college wants to have in a classroom with other students. And the essays are a window into what each applicant may contribute to that classroom discussion.

What about some final advice for writing college application essays?

Do spend time brainstorming with your parents, advisors or mentors about what you plan to write, what you have written, and what you will rewrite.

Basically, this is a marketing project – presenting yourself in the best possible (yet truthful) light for the intended college.

For extra help, you might consider the reader-friendly book "Made to Stick: Why Some Ideas Survive and Others Die" by Chip Heath and Dan Heath. The book's recommendations for making ideas sticky – ideas that people will remember and act on – are also very good for writing college essays.

The book describes the six principles of what the authors call SUCCESs – simple, unexpected, concrete, credible, emotional, stories. If you read the book for the explanation of these concepts, you will learn good life skills for both oral and written communication.

HAVE AN OPEN MIND. If the essay you wrote just does not seem to fit the bill (namely, what the essay question asks), be willing to start all over again from scratch.

GOING THE EXTRA MILE ON WRITING YOUR ESSAYS MAY MAKE A HUGE DIFFERENCE IN WHETHER YOU ARE ACCEPTED AT A PARTICULAR COLLEGE.

Write the absolute best essays you can.

EARLY ADMISSION OPTIONS

What is the deal with early admission options?

First, what does **early** mean? Early means that the deadline for your application is earlier – sometimes by as much as two to three months – from the regular admission deadline. For example, a college might have an early deadline of November 1 or November 15 while the regular deadline might be the end of December or the end of January or even later.

Make sure you read the early admission deadlines correctly.

With all the deadlines of which you have to keep track, the early deadlines can become blurred. Check and double check that you have the correct early deadlines for THIS YEAR'S admission process.

What is the advantage of turning in your application early?

Colleges that have an early deadline option report to the students several months before these same colleges report to students who apply for the regular deadline option. In other words, if you apply early to a college that has an early application option, you may have an answer sometime in December. If you apply regular admission to the same college, you may not hear until April, depending on that college's reporting date for regular admission.

What does deferred mean?

You may apply for the early admission option, and the answer you get back in December may be that you are **deferred**. This means that you are put into the regular admission pool of candidates for reconsideration.

Some colleges may have a "one-time or you are out" policy – if you are not accepted during the early admission pool you cannot be reconsidered during the regular deadline pool of candidates.

Read the application policies of each school carefully (the current application year's policies) to consider the best options for your application.

Besides knowing months before other reporting dates, what is the advantage of applying early?

You are making a strong statement that you really, truly want to go to this college. This helps admissions officers who want a good grasp on how many students who get accepted are likely to actually attend.

From a marketing point of view, colleges want to say "I do" to students who will reply "I do."

This is why students who opt for the early admission options are usually more sought after – because they are making a stronger commitment to saying "I do."

And thus students may decide to apply early because they hope to better their chances at being accepted.

What factors are important to consider in applying early?

The most important factor probably concerns financial aid. You need to read the college website information and probably check with the admissions office to be very, very clear on the financial aid policies.

For example, some colleges may have an early admission option that is binding. This means you contractually agree to attend the college if you are accepted early. But how does this affect financial aid? What if you are accepted and do not get the financial aid you need to attend?

You need to be very clear on how financial aid works at any college to which you apply early.

Colleges can and do change their early admission options.

Which colleges offer which early admissions options can change. Therefore you cannot assume that the options offered even the previous year are the same for the year you are applying. You must carefully check what are the current admission options for the year to which you are applying.

Check a college's student athlete policy regarding early admission.

If you are a student athlete and want to play on a college team (as opposed to a college club) and you want to apply early, you must check out that college's student athlete policy. For example, that college may not be able to guarantee before you apply early that you will get a spot on the water polo team if you are accepted. And you could be accepted early in an option that is binding and not get a spot on the water polo team.

If having a spot on a college water polo team is important, you may decide it is a better strategic plan for you to apply regular admission to several colleges with water polo teams so that you can increase your chances of having a spot on a college water polo team. Finding out this information will be part of your research.

Do all schools have early admission options?

Do not assume every school has early admission options. Some schools may only have a regular deadline and some may have **rolling admissions** where applications are reviewed as they are submitted.

Also carefully review whether an early admission option is binding.

Check the information on the website very carefully and, if in any doubt, speak to the admissions office.

How should you decide whether to apply early if your first-choice college has early admission options?

There is no cut-and-dried answer to this question because the early admission process often requires finessing – taking into consideration as many variables as possible including the all-important financial aid question.

Ask an adult for help with your application strategy.

If you want to apply early – how can you decide before the beginning of November of your senior year which college is your number one choice?

If you do your research early enough in your high school career and, if possible, visit your top choices at the end of your junior year rather than trying to squeeze in the visits at the beginning of your senior year, you should be prepared to make a well-informed decision by November.

Perhaps you have a number one choice, which makes early admission easy to say yes to if the school has this option (and you are comfortable with the financial aid situation).

Or perhaps, by September of your senior year, you like three equally. If you really want to improve your odds of getting into at least one of those three colleges, you may decide to choose one to apply to early if the option is available (and the financial aid situation is acceptable).

And, when you are applying early to only one college, you can authentically write an essay that College X is the one you really, truly, cross-my-heart-and-hope-to-die want to attend. (It is hard to write such an impassioned essay when applying regular decision because it is assumed at this point that you are applying to other colleges too.)

One more time, because it is so important, be very careful about the financial aid situation before deciding to apply early.

OTHER COLLEGE APPLICATION FACTORS

What is the word legacy mean in connection to college applications?

Legacy means that some colleges count it favorably if one of your parents (and sometimes one of your grandparents) attended the college. How much each college counts this factor depends on each college.

Ask the college's alum office if a legacy only counts for early options.

If you are applying to a college for which you have a legacy and the college is big on legacy applicants – find out if the legacy weighs favorably **only** for early admission applications (assuming this is an option at that college) or does a legacy also weigh favorably if you apply regular admission?

If you apply early to a school where you have a legacy, you are definitely stating you want to go to this school. If you apply regular decision to a college where you have a legacy, the admissions committee might think you are only applying to Mom or Dad's alma mater as a fallback if you do not get in where you really want to go. And remember that college admission officers have their eyes on the potential number of accepted students who will say yes to their acceptance.

What is the Common Application?

This is a standardized application for undergraduate college admission from the not-for-profit **Common Application** membership association, and this standardized application is accepted by many colleges. The colleges who do accept the Common Application are committed to treating an applicant using it the same as an applicant using the college's own individual application. (Some schools ask for supplemental material and essays besides the Common Application.)

Check out www.commonapp.org (note the **two** ps) to find out more about which colleges accept this application, which colleges also require additional material (supplements), and which of these colleges have early application options. And, as always, make sure you are looking at the current year's information.

From a strategic marketing perspective, if you are applying in an early admission option, you may want to use that college's own application even if the college also accepts the Common Application in order to emphasize this is truly the college you want to attend. (Obviously, if the college only uses the Common Application, you would use that application.)

Are there good reasons for NOT using the Common Application if you are applying regular admission to several schools, many of which accept the Common Application? This is a judgment call based on your time constraints and other factors, including the essay questions on the Common Application compared to the essay questions for the specific college applications.

From a strategic marketing perspective it seems to me rather hard to write a convincing essay that College X is your number one choice even though you are applying regular admission and submitting the Common Application to College X. Do think about this when you consider whether to use the Common Application.

One strategy would be to use an individual college application for the college or colleges you most want to attend, while using the Common Application for your other school choices.

And it may be that some supplement requirements are so numerous that it is just as convenient to use that college's own application rather than the Common Application and the college's supplement requirements.

What about the Universal College Application?

The Common Application has competition for a standardized application from the for-profit **Universal College Application** (www.universalcollegeapp.com) (again note the **two** ps). Check the differences in 1) which schools accept which application forms and, perhaps more importantly, 2) the differences in the way the information on these application forms can be used for various colleges. One system may work better for your needs than the other system.

Check out the essays on the two standardized applications.

If the schools to which you are applying regular admission take both standardized applications, you may consider choosing the one whose essay(s) and format most appeal to you.

What about on-campus interviews?

One way to demonstrate a real interest in a school is to visit the school. Some schools collect the names of students who take the official campus tours. Even if the school did not collect your name, when you write your essay about why you want to attend that school, you can weave into the essay what you saw and did while on campus.

(If you cannot afford to visit a school because of the distance from your hometown, do NOT assume this means that you will not be accepted. You can include in your application the information as to why you did not visit and then add why, from all your research about the school, you really want to attend this college.)

If you visit a school, there is the question of an on-campus interview. Many schools do not offer this option. Some schools offer it for students who have legacies, in which case the interviews may be run out of the alumni office and not out of the admissions office.

Get an on-campus interview if available.

If you visit the school and you can have an interview, do so. This is one more opportunity to demonstrate a genuine interest in the school. Remember to arrange ahead of time for an interview rather than just popping in unannounced and hoping someone has time to talk to you.

If the college website says interviews are not offered on campus, call the school to ask for yourself. You may discover you fit into a category of applicants who can get an interview on campus. Or, as one high school senior applying to a specialized program discovered, the directors of that program like to interview students on campus if the students show the initiative to ask for an interview. (But this opportunity is not revealed on the college's website.)

What about alumni interviews?

Other schools offer or require students be interviewed in their hometown by alumni living in that town.

Have an alumni interview if it is offered.

Take this interview even if it is not mandatory. You are going to write an essay why you want to attend the school. It is a good idea to talk to an alum about the school for information to turn into ideas for your essays. (**Caution:** If the alum graduated several years ago, do not assume that the information he/she tells you is still accurate.

You must still do your own due diligence.) Plus taking the time for this interview helps demonstrate your sincere interest in the school.

Alumni interviewers may have no training in interviewing.

In many cases these alumni have not been trained to conduct a college applicant interview. And some of them have been out of school 20 or more years and have not even been back for homecoming. They may not have the foggiest idea how to conduct an interview or be able to give you accurate answers to your questions.

Rule #1: DO NOT base your impression of the school on this alumni interview in your hometown.

Rule #2: DO NOT PANIC IF YOU THINK THE ALUMNI INTERVIEW DID NOT GO WELL.

Remember that these alumni interviewers are volunteers who are trying to help their alma mater get good college applicants. The alumni interviewers' motives are well-meaning even if their interview skills are lacking.

Alumni interviews are usually not a major decision factor.

In many cases these interviews are basically to ascertain that you are a human being. Word has it that at some schools the interviewer's comments only make a difference in two cases: the incredible candidates (the school would be foolish not to take this student) or the abysmal candidates (no one would be this student's roommate). For the rest the interview is more a courtesy to the student.

At other schools the notes of the alum interviewer may be considered during discussions of your application. You want to try to ensure that those notes are positive even if the interviewer does not know how to conduct an interview.

How can you help ensure a positive report by an alum interviewer?

Help the interviewer to interview you by: 1) being prepared to offer information about yourself or 2) ask questions that can get the conversation rolling.

Have two copies of your resume with you.

If the conversation gets stuck, hand one copy of the resume to the interviewer and use the other copy yourself for a prompt if performance nerves make you forget that incredible science project you did in 11th grade. And, yes, it is appropriate to talk about your achievements as long as this is in a professional context. This is **not** bragging as you may have been taught never to do. This is describing activities or achievements relevant to the interview.

Another use for the resume is if, at the end of the interview, you are concerned that the interviewer did not learn enough about you. As you are saying good-bye and thanking the interviewer for his/her time, hand the interviewer your resume "for a little more information."

Always answer in full sentences – avoiding "yes" and "no."

What kind of questions should you ask an interviewer?

Just as you should not answer questions with only a "yes" or "no," do **not** ask questions that can be answered by a yes or no.

Ask open-ended questions – these can rev up a conversation.

Check out the following example of the use of open-ended questions in an imagined alum interview at a local Starbucks:

Alum interview at a local Starbucks

(Example in which the admission candidate must help out an inexperienced interviewer.)

Alum: I'm Charles King. I graduated in 1985.

Candidate: I'm Susan Connor.

Alum: Pleased to meet you.

(The candidate smiles and then there is silence. The candidate now offers some information about herself.)

Candidate: I'm interested in College X because I understand that the fine arts department has exceptional teachers.

Alum: I majored in business. Never saw the inside of a fine arts classroom.

Candidate: The university also has a fine arts museum that is highly regarded.

Alum: Yeah, we visited it during freshmen orientation.

Candidate: During freshmen orientation do students visit many parts of the university?

Alum: Actually, I don't know what the current freshmen orientation schedule is. It's been a long time since I graduated.

(The candidate now takes the interview firmly into her own hands.)

Candidate: What were your favorite things about attending College X?

Alum: I loved the football games. My fraternity brothers and I would all get together beforehand and ….

(The candidate has managed to get the alum talking about something that interests him. The conversation is finally off and running. Note that it is not important whether the candidate is actually interested in the football games. The goal is to help the interviewer have a pleasant conversation.)

And if the interviewer then asks if you have any questions about the school, you should have prepared in advance well thought-out questions that are as specific as possible to this particular school.

Remember, asking what kind of exercise facilities are available or a question that is answered clearly on the website – such as whether the school has the major that interests you – does not present you in the best light. Do your homework before an alum interview so that you can ask thoughtful questions that the interviewer will probably be able to answer, such as "How active is the alumni association in this city?"

What other things should you know about your college applications?

Read all the fine print on the applications. Sometimes it is the fine print that can make the difference. If at the very end of an application you are offered to attach something you want to share, do so!

Show off your talent or passion.

If you are a writer, perhaps attach two pages of your best writing (probably the first two pages of a story or play rather than an engaging scene in the middle of the work). If you are an artist or aspiring architect or photographer, attach drawings or sketches or photographs.

Caution: For example, attaching photos you took in Paris on a summer trip would probably not be that interesting unless you took very, very artistic photographs because your goal is to major in photography.

Think outside the box as to what you can attach.

What application pitfalls should you try to avoid?

A high school senior turned in her requests for college recommendations to her high school college counselor by the high school's early September deadline as required. Two weeks later she learned that the college to which she planned to apply early – and whose soccer coach wanted her for the team – required a recommendation from a math teacher and an English teacher and not a recommendation from a history teacher and an English teacher as she had requested of her high school. The high school senior told her parents she could not now apply early to the college because she would not have a recommendation from a math teacher.

DO NOT GIVE UP SO EASILY!

Look for ways to make things work for you.

In this case, the high school wanted the requests early to make it easier on the school and the teachers. Yet, as plenty of time remained before the recommendation had to be sent, the student could go directly to her math teacher, explain the situation, and ask for a recommendation.

Then if the teacher said no, the student could contact the college and explain what happened due to her high school's rigid recommendation policy deadline. Not having a recommendation from her math teacher, given that she explained the situation to the college (and if she meets all the other application requirements), will probably not be a reason for the college to turn her down, especially a college where the soccer coach wants her for the team.

Ask politely for things you need for your college applications.

Some things are out of your control, such as whether the teacher will agree to write the recommendation. It is in your control to ask for the recommendation. (Of course you will ask politely with a smile rather than demanding the recommendation.)

If you come up against a similar obstacle, think outside of the box and try to figure out how to overcome the problem. And if you need advice, ask for help from parents, advisors or mentors.

Are there other opportunities to showcase your talents?

If you have talents that the schools to which you are applying might be interested in, do **not** only rely on the application to get the information across.

Let's say you are a percussionist interested in playing for the college marching band.

If you're going to be on campus – check ahead of time if you can arrange an appointment with the marching band director. If you get to meet the marching band director, this enables you to become a person rather than just an application. Meeting you gives the band director the opportunity to assess what a terrific addition you would make to the band. Plus you may be asked to demonstrate your ability on the snare drums or the timpani.

If you cannot visit the campus or the band director will be away when you visit – talk to the band director on the phone and offer to send a demo CD of your percussion abilities directly to the director or provide a link to a YouTube video, for example, on which the band director can watch you perform. And you can demonstrate your team band spirit by assuring the director that you will be happy to be flexible about which percussion instruments you play in the marching band.

Use this same strategy whatever your talent happens to be.

This same strategy applies to a sports talent, singing talent, art talent, or academic talent. Use the college's website to identify who might be interested in briefly meeting with you on campus or talking to you on the phone. Then contact that person or persons to set up in-person or phone appointments.

It is probably better to send an email first if you have the person's email address (colleges often list emails for professors and staff on the website) in order to explain BRIEFLY why you would like to meet/talk with the person. (Please, please use correct formal grammar and spelling in this email.)

If you want to set up an on-campus appointment, this can be done through email without taking up the person's time on the phone. Or if you are only planning to speak on the phone, then using email to set up a convenient time works well.

If you do not get an answer to your email, do not give up. Emails sometimes go into spam filters or disappear into thin air. You can call as a second step, keeping in mind when the college is on quarter, semester or summer break.

Also keep in mind, for example, that even if you are not the lead singer in your school's choir, there may be many singing choirs on a large campus that would be interested in having you as a member. Do your homework – yes, more research – to find out from the website or college materials which singing groups are on campus. Then contact the one or ones that you think are the best fit with your ability.

A strategy of "meet and greet" includes professors.

This strategy includes arranging to meet or speak with a professor with whom you might be interested in doing an undergraduate research project. Check the college website to see if you can find a professor whose research field is something that interests you. If that information is not available on the website, call the undergraduate admissions office. You may be transferred from person to person until you find your answer – remember it is important to practice polite persistence in getting information you want.

And these "meet and greet" suggestions are relevant whether you want to play on a college sports team, write for the college award-winning newspaper, or participate in any specific college activity where talent or passion is required.

The point of "meet and greet" is a note to the admissions office.

The main point in all this effort – yes, effort, and remember the goal – is to have the person you meet/talk with send a note to the admissions office of that person's interest in you. You do not necessarily ask for this note; you simply place yourself in the position where the person may take the initiative after meeting or talking with you.

Even if the person does not send a note on his/her own, you can mention in one of the essays for this college that you met/talked with this professor/staff person and you are very interested in playing percussion in the marching band or singing in a specific college choir. First, this demonstrates real interest and initiative on your part. Second, the admissions office may contact the person you met/ spoke with and presumably you will then be given a good recommendation by that person.

And speaking of recommendations …

HE SAID, SHE SAID – THE IMPORTANT RECOMMENDATIONS

What recommendations?

Many colleges will ask for the guidance counselor or high school college counselor or the English teacher or whoever to write a recommendation for you.

Carefully consider when you are given a choice.

When you are given a choice of teachers, carefully consider which teacher or teachers would most support how you have positioned yourself in your application – serious music student, talented athlete, literature-lover. While it is nice to have a recommendation from a teacher who really likes you, if that teacher can only recommend you in a general way (great homeroom student), consider a teacher who can recommend you in a specific – and positive – way (for example, did the lion's share of creating the scenery for all high school productions).

Give the person plenty of time before the deadline.

With careful planning, you can give a person from whom you have asked for a recommendation plenty of time to write it. It is totally unrealistic to ask a teacher only a few days before the deadline to write a recommendation for you. It is a good idea to put in your requests for recommendations at the very beginning of your college application process.

Provide your resume to a teacher as a recommendation aid.

When you ask a teacher for a recommendation, provide him/her with a copy of your resume. Your teacher may have no idea that you are as interesting out of class as you are in class.

You may also, if you feel the teacher will not take it amiss, provide him/her with talking points for the recommendation. Talking points are what you would like emphasized in the recommendation if appropriate – and the points may be different for different schools.

For example, you may want your creative writing ability emphasized for a college that is known to be looking for creative writers, while you want your singing ability emphasized for a college that is known to be looking for choral members.

Another example of talking points might include (if true) the out-of-the-box ideas you contribute in class that enhance the classroom discussions.

Give the deadline date for the recommendation.

Make sure you give the person writing the recommendation the deadline date for the recommendation. (Or perhaps give a somewhat earlier date just to be safe. Then on that earlier date check politely that the recommendation has been submitted. If it has not, the person can quickly write a recommendation that will meet the actual deadline.)

EXTRA HOMEWORK

What else can you do to stand out in the application process?

Now let's talk about another category of recommendations: **the ones for which universities do not specifically ask**. That's right, the ones **not** asked for. These can be more important than the required ones.

(There are some colleges that do not accept extra recommendations. If extra recommendations are specifically NOT banned, then assume they are allowed. But do read all the application rules very, very carefully.)

To illustrate what I am talking about, let me tell you this story. One spring day I walked into Starbucks and spotted an acquaintance. I asked her whether her son – we'll call him Jon – got into NYU's Tisch School of the Arts. The son had been a professional actor since a young age and his resume included a role as the on-screen child of a major movie star.

The mother said, "He's on the waiting list." I said, "Get him off the waiting list."

Then I remembered that in another film project her son had acted with a well-known adult actor who graduated from Tisch. "Get a recommendation from this actor," I said.

The mother admitted that she had not done this before when Jon applied – she was nervous about asking (the actor could have just said no). Now the mother would ask for a recommendation.

I do not know how many applicants got off the waiting list that year -- Jon was one of them. He had the legitimate talent along with the luck to have as a contact an actor grad of Tisch happy to write a recommendation that could truly benefit Jon.

This is the kind of recommendation I am talking about. The ones written by people who have known you since you were in kindergarten or the ones written by graduates of the school you are applying to who have seen you in action or for whom you have done an internship or worked.

One young woman worked in a lawyer's office the summer before 12th grade when she planned to apply to Yale as her first choice college. This young woman's goal was to be a lawyer (she is one now) and the lawyer with whom she purposely interned was a Yalie. What kind of recommendation do you think she got?

Yes, she had other things going for her when she applied to Yale. Yet that recommendation was probably a valuable part of her application. And she gained the recommendation while learning about a career path that interested her. (FYI – For this particular summer job the young woman worked more hours than expected of her. I am sure this going-the-extra-mile effort helped earn her a stellar recommendation.)

My younger daughter, through a serendipity sequence of events, asked for (note the words "asked for") and got a summer internship with the literary manager of a major Los Angeles theater. When my daughter applied to the University of Pennsylvania, she was delighted to learn that the literary manager had written in the recommendation that the literary manager's interns were usually grad students or at least college students. My daughter had been the first high school student intern, and the recommendation said she had done as well as the older interns.

Seeking out these internships is a subject I cover in more depth in the next book in this series – HOW TO SUCCEED IN COLLEGE

AND PREP FOR BEYOND COLLEGE. The examples here are to get you thinking – to show you the kinds of recommendations you can legitimately go after to add to your applications.

One more example: When I found out the right-hand person of my nephew's father was an alum of a school to which he was planning to apply, I suggested my nephew get a recommendation from her. Oh no he said, what could she say? I said that the recommendation was not to talk about his academic abilities but simply (and yet importantly) be a personal recommendation. The right-hand person could say that she had known him since he was a baby and what a fine young man he turned out to be.

Social media tip: If, for example, you have been very active on an appropriate LinkedIn group, adding valuable comments to several discussion threads, you might ask for someone active in those same discussions to recommend you. Just because someone has never physically met you does not mean he/she cannot recommend you.

Get personal recommendations from family friends if appropriate.

How do you ask for recommendations?

When contacting someone by email to ask for a recommendation for college, be careful to clearly state what you are asking. Here is a sample of an **unclear** recommendation email request:

Dear Mrs. Thomas:

I am beginning to apply to colleges and as part of the process I need recommendations. I would appreciate it very much if you would write one for me.
Attached is a resume with personal information.

What is the problem with this request?

It is not specific enough. Which are the colleges for which the recommendation will be used? This is needed to allow the writer to craft the recommendation for the specific school.

Perhaps the writer is an alum of the school and will say so in the recommendation. Or perhaps the recommendation writer knows something about the specific school that can be incorporated to make the recommendation stronger.

The student may have sent this out now before deciding which colleges to apply to because the student heard it was important to ask for recommendations early in the application cycle.

If the student wanted to ask early in the cycle, a better approach would be a heads up approach until the student decided on specific colleges to which to apply.

Here is an example of what could be written now:

Dear Mrs. Thomas:

I will be applying to colleges this fall, and I would very much appreciate a recommendation from you. If this is okay with you, I will get back to you when I have the specific colleges.

At that time, I will also email you a copy of my resume for background information.

Regards,
High School Student

By asking early and getting a yes response, the student has in effect reserved a future recommendation. When the student is ready for the recommendation to be written, the student can supply the names of the specific schools. Thanks to computers, it is easy for the writer to use the same recommendation for several schools and yet mention the specific school in each recommendation.

Additional tip: In considering your overall application, you might want to request certain information in specific recommendation letters. Thus you might ask Mrs. Thomas if she is comfortable mentioning how much your ideas contributed to the discussions of the Meetup group to which you belong. And you might ask another person if he would discuss how you took the initiative in your junior year of high school to start a tutoring program in a nearby elementary school.

CONNECTING TO OTHER PEOPLE FOR HELP

When you are looking for help with recommendations or internships or whatever you may need in connection with following your path, you probably will not already know all the people who can help you.

You will need to go outside your circle of friends and acquaintances to find people who can help you.

Have you ever played the Kevin Bacon trivia game?

According to Wikipedia: "The trivia game **Six Degrees of Kevin Bacon** is based on a variation of the concept of the small world phenomenon which states that any actor can be linked, through their film roles, to Kevin Bacon." Wikipedia uses the following example of connecting Elvis Presley and Kevin Bacon: "Elvin Presley was in *Change of Habit* (1969) with Edward Asner. Edward Asner was in *JFK* (1991) with Kevin Bacon."

This game illustrates the saying that everyone is connected to everyone else by six degrees of separation. (John Guare wrote the play "Six Degrees of Separation" that was made into a movie of the same name. If you want to know more about this concept, read chapter 2 of Malcolm Gladwell's book "The Tipping Point.")

The trick is finding the connections. First, we will do this the old-fashion way:

For example, if I want to find a connection to a certain writer on a television drama show and I do not know anyone else working on that show, I could look up the writer's credits on www.imdb.com. Then I could click on each of the other shows for which that writer has written to check the credits for those shows. Let's say I recognize a name of another writer whom I know has a sister that works out at my gym. Then I have to find someone at my gym to introduce me to the sister of that writer, and then get that writer to introduce me to the writer I originally wanted to meet.

Put in the effort in order to get the results.

Yes, it is complicated and it does not always work. For example, the sister may say no to me. Then I have to keep looking for another connection -- or give up. Yet, if the person you want to contact is someone you really, really want to meet, it is worth the effort to see if you can follow a trail of connections to that person.

Now let's look at an example using social media sites. Imagine I want to connect with a lawyer who works at a law firm in Los Angeles. I go to the firm's website and read about the lawyer, and I discover that he graduated from the University of Pennsylvania's law school. His email is given on the law firm's site, but I want to see if I have a connection to him before I email him cold.

Next I go to LinkedIn.com and search by company on his law firm's name. He is listed as one of the firm's lawyers who is in my network on LinkedIn so I can click through to his LinkedIn profile. On his profile I learn that he is a member of the University of Pennsylvania Alumni LinkedIn group, of which I am also a member. Now when I email him at his law firm, I can mention that connection as a way of warming up the cold email.

How do you follow a trail of connections?

Remember back in an earlier section of the book when I suggested keeping track of your parents' friends' colleges and careers and the same for your friends' parents? This is where you review all those notes you have and use the Internet to research these people and their online connections.

For some of you it may appear that your family and friends do not have any connections to people who, for example, might be able to write a recommendation to a particular school.

Think again – and again.

Put on your ol' thinking cap and toss around names.

Yes, toss around names with whoever will brainstorm with you. Then see what you come up with.

And, remember, if you want things to happen for yourself, it is always a good idea to make things happen for others (without expecting anything in return).

Social media tip: *If someone asks a question on a social media site on which you participate and you can answer the question,* *do so. You need to be willing to help others if you want others to help you.*

Help others figure out to whom they can connect.

Or while you are brainstorming for yourself, if you happen to come up with a possibility for a friend whom you know is looking for that kind of recommendation, share the info with the friend. And when someone unexpectedly helps you, you will definitely feel deserving of that help.

SUMMER PROGRAMS VS. SUMMER PROGRAMS – SOME YOU PAY FOR

In considering the all-important summer before 12th grade and how best to maximize your time, you should carefully consider possibilities. And, sometimes, having tons of money can hurt rather than help you. This is because it is important, besides the specific activity, to show INITIATIVE.

What are some examples of activities for the summer before 12th grade?

Let's say your parents have plenty of money so you plan to go to Europe for the summer and write your major college application essay on the art you saw in Rome. Nice, but you did not do anything on your own to achieve that end. Your parents gave you the money and you got on a plane.

Now suppose, for example, you learn of a program in Rome that is fee-based but you can only attend if you are one of 12 students from the entire United States selected on the basis of an essay on the works of the Italian Baroque painter Caravaggio. You apply, and lo and behold, you are one of the 12 people selected! Now you write a college application essay about your art experience that is much more impressive because you include the information that you earned the right to attend based on your passion and talent.

And a third imaginary scenario – there is a competition for American high school art students painting in the style of Caravaggio. In this case 12 students are selected for an all-expenses-paid trip to Rome to study Caravaggio's paintings and you are one of these 12 students. This is also very impressive.

Carefully consider your summer activities.

Think through what kinds of experiences you want to have in this all-important summer.

And, yes, there are more and more programs catering to high school students in which, for example, the students spend the summer in South America building houses for impoverished families. Yet, again, these are programs that are often selective only by virtue of who gets their application (and fees) in first. While this is community service, everything has been arranged for you. Instead, consider what community service projects you could do that you would arrange for yourself.

Do two different activities in one summer.

Another point to remember is that summer vacation is usually three months long. You can do an internship for part of the summer and participate in a second program the other part of the summer.

If you need to work, get the most from that activity.

And for those of you who must work during the summer – you can write an effective essay describing that you had to work and what you learned from the experience. (Remember, write about specifics not generalities. For example, write not that you learned to give good customer service but instead write about a specific example of good customer service that you performed.) Then, if besides your paying job you can squeeze in a small amount of time for a short internship or a volunteer project, this clearly demonstrates the type of hard-working person you are.

Pay attention to the deadlines for competitive programs.

Deadlines for competitions and programs come early. You need to research program possibilities online, at the library, and at local bookstores in the fall of junior year in order to plan for the following summer.

(There may even be, for example, competitive official state art programs, and these programs may have subsidized fees. In California, one terrific program is the California State Summer School for the Arts – www.csssa.org – for California residents and a limited number of out-of-state students.)

Prepare and submit your applications as soon as the applications become available. You do not want to wait to the last minute to apply when all the spaces might be filled (as in rolling admission programs) or you accidentally miss the deadline by one day.

Use the advice elsewhere in this book to ensure that you write effective essays, get good recommendations, and overall present yourself in a positive (although truthful) light.

Get competitive program applications in early.

ADDITIONAL ASSISTS IN COLLEGE APPLICATIONS

Can sports be a possible assist into college? (Do not automatically skip this section.)

A college may be interested in you for the sport you play even if you are not a widely recruited football or basketball high school star.

At various U.S. colleges today there are many college sports teams (as opposed to college sports clubs) in addition to football and basketball **whose coaches may have a say in your acceptance at the college**.

Some of these sports may be fencing, tennis, swimming, lacrosse, track, golf; schools may have women's teams in some sports and men's teams in other sports.

And your own high school coach may be able to recommend you to the college coach.

Play sports because you love it or it is what you want to learn.

Do **not** participate in high school sports only as something to put on your college application. If you are **not** interested in sports, spend your limited free time pursuing something you love.

Where can you learn which schools have which college teams?

Check out the National Collegiate Athletic Association's website at www.ncaa.org for information on how student athletes can comply with NCAA bylaws in order to compete in intercollegiate athletics as well as information on what high school students need to do to be eligible to compete their first year in college.

If you are planning to visit a campus with a college sports team on which you would be interested in playing, contact the coach ahead of time for a possible appointment. You can ask your high school coach to put in a good word for you with the college coach.

Contact the coach ahead of an on-campus visit.

If you and the college coach hit it off, it is quite possible that the coach will notify the admissions office that he/she is interested in you (although this does not necessarily mean you will be accepted nor does it necessarily mean a sports scholarship). If the team could use your ability and you want to play on the team, you might thus find yourself in a stronger applicant position.

Telling a coach you will play on the team is an implied contract.

If you tell a college coach that you will be a member of his/her team if you are accepted to the college and then attend, in my opinion this is an implied contract. This is especially so if the college coach has put in a good word for you with the admissions office.

It is a serious commitment that you should keep for at least one season of your sport. If you have no intention of participating in that sport once you get to college, you should **not** tell a college coach you will participate in order to get the coach to help with your application.

This is an important life lesson – only make commitments that you intend to keep. The trustworthiness of your word is a very important attribute for success in life. You want to earn the reputation of someone who can be trusted.

A coach putting in a good word for you that helps get you into that college is the same as a debt (like car payments). You pay back the debt to the coach with sweat equity – your time and effort – rather than in money payments for the car. And you have a responsibility to pay off the debt before you join a fraternity or sorority or undertake other activities that interfere with your commitment to the coach.

Play sports wholeheartedly – be the best you can be.

STANDARDIZED TESTS

A word about the SATs or the ACTs

For college entrance exams -- go to www.collegeboard.com for SAT tests or www.act.org for ACT tests. The two standardized tests measure different abilities and/or knowledge, and high schools in some areas of the country favor one test over the other.

Standardized tests are only one part of your overall application.

Check with the colleges to which you plan to apply to ensure that either test is acceptable for your application. Then if you have a choice and you know which of the two tests plays to your strengths, choose to take that test.

(**Important note:** There are colleges that do **not** require any standardized tests. If standardized tests are difficult for you and thus do not demonstrate your true abilities, do research online to find these colleges.)

You can improve your test scores by studying for these tests.

It helps to get comfortable with the way the test questions are asked and answered. You can take a preparatory course in person or online or practice diligently on your own or with a buddy.

Pothole alert: Be careful if someone offers you an old SAT or ACT practice book. You have to make sure you are using an SAT or ACT test book that includes the most recent test changes as these tests do change over the years.

Which SAT Subject Tests (formerly called Achievement Tests or SAT IIs) should you take?

Check which SAT Subject Tests are required for each college to which you apply. The SAT Subject Tests required, for example, for the University of California schools may be different than those for other schools.

This can be an important difference:

For example, if you are required for a specific college application to take an SAT Subject Test in a subject in which you do not shine, do not use that SAT Subject Test for another college application that does **not** require that specific test.

Yes, you may have to take more SAT Subject Tests using this strategy. Yet you can increase your chances of acceptance by reporting SAT Subject Tests in which you do shine. (In other words, do not be lazy and take the minimum of the required SAT Subject Tests if those three are not in your strongest academic areas. Take additional SAT Subject Tests that are in your strongest academic areas.)

Here is more information on the different SAT Subject Tests - - http://sat.collegeboard.org/practice/sat-subject-test-preparation

Pay attention to each college's specific required SAT Subject Tests.

GET ALL THE INFORMATION YOU CAN ON EACH COLLEGE

Should you attend the local area presentations given by colleges that interest you?

Absolutely.

First, talks given by college representatives at your high school or at a city-wide presentation are one way to learn about required SAT

Subject Tests (if the application does not make this clear) and other peculiarities of different schools.

Even if you have heard the talk about a specific school your junior year, it is wise to hear the talk again in your senior year. You never know when that one tiny piece of new information – mentioned by the second presenter but not by the first or a change in policy between the two years – is the one piece of information that makes all the difference in your application.

Pan for nuggets of gold wherever and whenever possible.

And whenever you are confused about something on a college application that you are filling out, call the university for clarification. MAKE SURE YOU TALK TO THE RIGHT PERSON. Frequently the left hand of any organization does not know what the right hand is doing.

Find the right person at the college to whom to talk.

If the question is important and you feel that the person you reached in the admissions office, for example, seemed unsure of the answer, call again to try to reach a different person. Call until you are sure you have the right answer.

A mother called the admissions office of a prestigious university about a question regarding her son's application for a specialized program of the university. The admissions person seemed tentative about the answer. The mother then called directly to the specialized program. Totally different answer. And this time the person provided additional valuable information that could help with the application.

Always be willing to ask for clarification.

FINANCIAL AID

Where is the money and who qualifies for it?

This is an immensely important topic, and one which is outside the scope of this book.

All kinds of easily available sources exist for advice on college financial aid. Just make sure you are looking at the most current information.

Googling "college financial aid."

You do have to use good consumer sense, though, because every financial aid offer is **not** equal. Different lenders have different conditions and different rates. And even sometimes the preferred lender list of the college to which you will be attending has to be considered with a critical eye.

Remember the saying "buyer beware" and act accordingly.

Do due diligence in your research and you may be surprised how high a family's income can be and still qualify for need-based financial aid. Plus there are merit awards and special interest awards and many other possibilities. You have to be willing to invest the time in order to increase the possibilities of reaping the award.

Keep an open mind about whether you qualify for financial aid.

And remember that a college's financial aid parameters can change every year. Although you may have been turned down one year, you may qualify the next year.

The following exercises may seem silly but they really do help.

EXERCISES

Exercise A:

1)   As a confidence booster, write a list of all the reasons your college application may be denied that have nothing to do with you,

such as the college admissions officer had a fight with his/her kid just before he/she read your application or the college admissions officer had a bad cold and could barely concentrate on what he/she reviewed. Remember to read this list every so often during the actual college application process so you keep a realistic perspective.

2)   Write a list of the areas of the country most interesting to you, considering both weather/climate (including allergy considerations) and urban/rural settings. Prioritize the list and then see if you can match a sample of colleges located in each area on your list.

3)   To think outside the box – make a list of some of your talents/skills. These are not school subjects necessarily; they can be as varied as "great at planning parties" to "I get my friends to agree when they all have different opinions." Now see if you can brainstorm with someone as to what kinds of careers would build on these skills. Once you have this second list, see if you can match a sample of colleges that offer majors or minors in the career areas you have listed. Where are the overlaps between the colleges with these majors or minors and the colleges in the locations that interest you?

Exercise B:

1)   To loosen up your essay writing muscles -- pick a very mundane topic, such as "What brand of potato chips I like best." Write a short (one-page double-spaced) essay that vividly brings to life this simple subject. (Note: You do not have to show this to anyone so feel free to be as creative as you want.)

2)   After you write the above essay, see if you can spot any spelling or grammar mistakes before you run spelling and grammar checks. Correct the mistakes you find; then run spelling and grammar checks to see if the computer picks up any others. Correct these. (Yes, I know no one is seeing this essay. The point is to learn to correct your own errors. We are trying to teach the brain to recognize common errors, and by focusing on correcting these helps put these potential errors in long-term memory.) Then read the essay aloud to see if you have used incorrect words, such as "site" when you meant "sight."

3)   Now write another short essay on a subject somewhat more weighty, such as "Why I like _____ (school subject area) the most of all my classes this year." Note: This can be because you like the subject area or you like the teacher's classroom style or you like the red-head sitting two rows in front of you. Again, the point is to feel free to be creative as no one will see this.

4)   You know what is coming now: Repeat step 2 for your second essay.

Exercise C:

1)   Script an interview conversation between you and an alum of a specific college. Choose a specific college that you know about even if you may not be interested in attending that college. The point here is to be able to script a dialogue based on realistic information. If you do not know about any specific college, go to any college's website and read the information. (If you do have a target school in mind, study that college's website.) Do not be easy on yourself. Write some hard questions, such as "I see from your resume you did not do anything the summer before 12th grade. Why is that?" (FYI: You better have a darn good reason -- such as knee surgery that put you out of commission all summer and you still could have taken an online college course -- for this important question. And the answer is not "I wanted to take it easy all summer." This response will not impress alumni interviewers looking for committed students.)

2)   Print out two copies of the script and enlist someone to take the role of the alum interviewer. Practice shaking hands with the "interviewer," maintaining good eye contact, posture, etc. Then the two of you read the script aloud, trying not to speak in a monotone or in a too-loud voice.

3)   If possible, audio or video record this practice interview. Review how you sound/look. Did you project confidence in yourself without overdoing it?

4)   Now ask your "interviewer" to ad lib an interview with you about the same college. (If possible audio or video record this too.) Note

whether you say "um" or "well" before each response. If so, practice mentally pausing without saying any filler words before replying. This is not a race to the finish line but a well-considered conversation. **Hostile interview question tip:** If the interviewer asks a question that truly throws you, you can reply: "That's a good question. I'll have to think about it. Perhaps we can get back to it at the end of our talk." (Assuming the question was not something such as "Why do you want to go to this college?" You had better know the answer to that one – and a well-considered answer – before you begin the interview.)

CHAPTER V: AFTER THE COLLEGE/PROGRAM APPLICATIONS ARE IN

You are on the home stretch. You have all your college or post-high school program applications in on time, and your standardized test scores and your recommendations are in. You have even had your alumni interview in your hometown.

Is there anything you can do now to enhance your candidacy?

Update your application if appropriate.

Usually there are several months between the deadline for a regular application and the acceptance reporting date by the university in the spring. Except in cases where contact with the admissions office is firmly discouraged, you have the opportunity during these months to blow your own horn if there are new updates.

Let colleges know when you have done something special.

What is an appropriate update? Obviously getting the best grade on a senior English paper is not something to report to the colleges or programs. On the other hand, if you win a city-wide essay contest and are then asked to write a speech for the mayor, this is definitely worth reporting.

Contact the universities to which you have applied and ask how best to officially notify them so that this information will be added to your application.

If you have something good to share, share it.

Keep in mind that colleges often ask for your first semester senior year high school report card if you are not applying early. (Sometimes colleges request mid-first semester progress reports for students applying early.) Thus your first-semester grades and courses may be added to your application.

And, yes, everyone has to keep up his or her grades all senior year. Colleges can request both first and second semester grade reports and have the right to withdraw an acceptance if you have blown your grades by going to the beach every day since you got your acceptance.

If you want to enhance your application, be creative in developing additional information that can improve your chances. For example, if when you applied to colleges you discovered a lack in one area (such as your leadership abilities or your volunteer efforts), contemplate how you might fill that gap now. (Yes, the college may realize you are purposely filling the gap. Yet, even so, this demonstrates initiative and a real desire to be accepted by that college.)

In addition, an event may have occurred in your school or hometown that provides an opportunity not previously existing. (For example, if a hurricane devastates a nearby town and you respond by organizing a humanitarian project, this opportunity did not exist beforehand.)

Is there anything else you should be doing in preparation for college or program acceptance?

Think about how you are going to spend next summer.

If you feel you have a deficiency in a skill needed for college, think about summer school after you graduate high school to help strengthen that deficiency. And, this is important to remember: that summer school grade does not ever need to be reported to anyone. If, for example, foreign languages are your weak link, and your college requires you take two years of a language, you might consider taking an intensive first-year language course during the summer after you graduate high school. Then when you take the first semester of that language in college, you will be better prepared to pass the course.

Or if writing essays throws you, take a community college or online writing course to help prepare for college. Many, many high school students with good grades in their English classes are not prepared for the writing analyses usually required in college. Give yourself a boost by taking a college-level course the summer before you have to take the real thing.

You may even want to take a cooking course if you are going to live in your own apartment. Or a car repair course. Or any course that can help with the next stage of your life.

(One such course might be a basic financial course. Understanding the consequences of the accumulation of credit card debt, the need to keep enough money in your checking account so as not to bounce checks, etc. could be very helpful in college and for the rest of your life.)

What about after you have gotten the results?

Scenario #1: You have gotten acceptances to some colleges and been put on the waiting list at your number one choice. What to do?

First, contact the university's admissions office at the college where you are waitlisted and report that you are still very much interested in attending. When a university has the opportunity to accept students off the waiting list, the university would rather accept a student who has confirmed he/she still wants to attend rather than a student who got the waitlist notification yet did not notify the school of continuing interest. (The university may not have requested an RSVP. It is up to you to take the initiative.)

If you have not given the school an update since your application – and you have appropriate new information to add to your application, let the school know. And, if you can come up with a new recommendation that might help, now is the time to go after it.

Scenario #2: You have gotten acceptances to some colleges although none of the ones you really wanted to attend.

Possible solution: Defer on the best acceptance you received (obtain permission to come the following year but note that not every college allows this) and take a year off to do something that could change your application picture. Then during that gap year -- reapply to colleges that said no to you (demonstrating continued interest) or to new colleges that now interest you while doing something that enhances your application.

Do try to get feedback from the colleges that did not accept you as to what were the weak links in your application. While this may not be possible, it is worth a try. If you do get an answer, you will have important knowledge for strengthening your application during your gap year.

What might you do during a gap year?

Now comes the brainstorming part of taking a year off before college.

Again, this does not mean you have to spend money to attend some fancy program. If you are determined, you can find something to demonstrate an ongoing interest in your passion area, for example, without breaking the bank.

Let's start with a program that does cost, and go from there:

- Attend a full-time university that will accept you and thus demonstrate you can do well in college-level courses. (Consider this even if the credits will not transfer back to your targeted acceptance college.) Perhaps do this in another country where you can also work on your foreign language ability.

- Participate in a humanitarian project.

- Start you own Internet business and demonstrate business initiative.

- Work full-time to earn money for college and take one evening community college course a semester in a subject whose weakness is revealed on your high school transcript.

You get the idea. And you have several months before the next year's college applications are due, so you could do more than one thing.

What about transferring?

There are some schools do not allow you to transfer in unless as a freshman. If you attended another university for a year and re-applied to this college and got accepted, you would have to start over again as a freshman. This may be okay if you truly want to attend this particular college.

Then there are schools that do not allow you to transfer in until you have junior standing with a specific number of credits.

Or there are the schools that allow you to transfer as a sophomore.

Check out the transfer requirements of various schools.

Before deciding to take a gap year and then reapply, check out the transfer information for your targeted colleges.

Another possibility: Attend summer school for credit at a particular college where you would like to be accepted. Doing well in this course or courses could help when you reapply along with demonstrating continuing interest in the school. And a bonus would be if you could get a a recommendation, consider other school activities during the summer in which you can participate. You never know who you may connect with via this activity.

What if all else fails?

If all else fails and you do not get into one of your top choice colleges, attend a college you did get into with a positive attitude.

Turn lemons into lemonade – and make it your favorite.

Dive right in and make the college you are attending the best possible experience for you in terms of education, friendships and future career goals. Get involved in campus activities, find friends with similar interests, and enjoy!

If you are worried about feelings of failure, read Carol Dweck's book "Mindset: The New Psychology of Success." This book may be just the tonic you need for regaining a positive attitude. (Actually, I recommend everyone – including your parents, mentors and advisors – read this incredibly powerful book.)

As soon as you check into your freshman dorm, start thinking ahead on how what you are doing at this college can be utilized for your next stage in life. With the right attitude you might discover that the college you are attending is actually the best one for you.

EXERCISES

Exercise A:

1)   Make a list of the types of activities you could do senior year of high school after your applications are in that could enhance your application status.

2)   Write a brief sample email to a specific college (pick one) describing one of these imaginary activities. Be creative and mentally design an unusual activity. Describe both the project and who benefits from it.

3)   Write an email to a college that has waitlisted you (pick a specific one) stating you are still very interested in attending and why you would be an asset to the college if accepted.

TIP: Let's talk about persuasive writing. The most important thing to remember is this: *To try to persuade someone to agree with your point of view, you must NOT write what you want to say to convince the person. You MUST write what the person needs to hear/read in order to agree with you.* In other words, you first have to give some thought to what might motivate the person to agree with you.

As an example, we will assume you are waitlisted at a college known for its interest in student applicants who are creative writers. Yet you are not a creative writer and your strongest ability is in organizing projects to help the homeless. If you only write the email about your strongest ability, you may not be offering anything in which the college is interested; after all, this info surely already appeared on your application.

Now imagine this in the email to the targeted college: "In my work with homeless children I have discovered a lack of writing skills due to their frequent absences from school. I have been working with these children to improve their writing. If accepted at _____, I would like to start an afterschool creative writing program at a homeless shelter to help these children." Of course you have to mean this. Yet this is a great example of building on your own strongest ability to meet the college's perceived interest. And the bonus? If you get accepted off the waitlist and actually start this program, your future resume for applying for internships, your first post-college job and grad school is definitely enhanced.

Exercise B:

1) Make a list of possible activities or programs you could do in a gap year between high school and college. Include both ones you would like to do and ones that you believe would help you reapply to your targeted school(s).

2) Take one of the more complicated ideas (not "get a job at the local pizzeria") and list the steps you might take to achieve this activity or program. You might use the idea of teaching English as a second language in China for six months without knowing Chinese. Research on the Internet and by talking to teachers and others how someone might apply for such a post and what the requirements are to get such a job.

3) Now to practice your own persuasive writing skills, write an essay that would accompany your re-application to College X. The essay should emphasize that you so much want to attend College X that you are reapplying and also emphasize the experiences you learned teaching English as a second language in China that could translate to something beneficial for the college. (Hint: Perhaps you could teach English as a second language to new immigrants in neighborhoods near the college. You can mention how the college could get the PR benefit of helping its local community.)

Exercise C:

1)   Here is the assignment for a potentially difficult task: Practice an imaginary dialogue with a friend (play both parts) in which you explain that you did not get into the college of your choice so you are planning to do _____ for the next year and then reapply. The reason this exercise can be difficult is because many people may have a fixed mindset as explained in Dweck's book "Mindset." Thus you may believe that not getting into the college of your choice is an embarrassing failure on your part. Now granted, if your grades and standardized test scores were way below what a particular college stated as its range of acceptance, then perhaps this should have been considered before you applied. Yet if your grades and standardized test scores were within range and you did not get in, remember what I said before: Your rejection could be something as simple as the admissions officer had a bad day and did not look fondly on the applications he/she read. Shake off that feeling of failure and practice saying in an imaginary conversation: "I did not get into the school I wanted to attend. It is still my first choice. I am going to defer going to college next year and see if I can increase my chances for the college to take me the following year." (And, if you do not get in the following year, yet you have had a growth gap year, you should be in a more positive mindset when you arrive at whichever college you actually attend.) Note: In the above example of what to say to a friend, no reason was given for why you did not get into the school. You simple state you did not get in without giving any reason (unless you actually know and want to reveal this). If your friend presses you as to why you did not get in, you still do not need to give excuses. You can simply reply, "I don't know."

2) Now if you did not get into the college you wanted to attend, say this speech to a real person. Afterwards, notice that the ground did not open up and swallow you whole. In addition, you have learned how powerful it can be to role play important conversations before actually having them.

In book 2 of this series – HOW TO SUCCEED IN COLLEGE AND PREP FOR BEYOND COLLEGE – we'll be looking at various skills for life as well as effectively using social media to position yourself for your life after college graduation.

And in book 3 – HOW TO SUCCEED BEYOND COLLEGE – we'll be looking at more useful information for adult life.

I hope this first book will help you do well in high school, and I look forward to sharing information to help you succeed in college and beyond.

Bonus: Check out on the next page the extra material I have included for you: a tip sheet to help you write dynamic college application essays.

Bonus: How to Use Dynamic Language on a College Application Essay

Summary:

Following a few basic recommendations helps the language of your essay sound dynamic rather than weak.

Introduction:

Some people mistakenly think that dynamic language in a college application essay means using those big words you memorized for the standardized tests. Actually, the opposite is true. Unfamiliar words interrupt a reader's thought process and can make him/her lose the train of thought.

What you want to do is use familiar words in a dynamic way that keeps the reader moving along at a good reading pace. Follow the rules below to increase the dynamic flow of your essay. (You are not expected to do all the following on a first or second draft. Do these steps for the stage we will call "the polish.")

Rule #1: Get rid of words that are unfamiliar to most readers. For example, do NOT say: She wrapped a scarf around her **florid face**. Instead say: She wrapped a scarf around her **ruddy face**. The word "florid," which is used less often than "ruddy," could interrupt a reader's thoughts.

119

Rule #2: Get rid of forms of the verb "to be." For example, do NOT say: **I am hoping** to see my brother in his orchestra recital. Instead say: **I hope** to see my brother in his orchestra recital. Notice how much more energy appears in the words "I hope" as opposed to the words "I am hoping." And, yes, sometimes following this rule will require an entire sentence be rewritten in order to get rid of a form of the verb "to be."

Rule #3: Get rid of all adverbs. For example, do NOT say: **I walked quickly** towards the airport exit gate. Instead say: **I strode** towards the airport exit gate. Go through your entire essay and eliminate the adverbs. Then choose stronger verbs that include the concept of the adverbs you eliminated.

Rule #4: Use descriptive adjectives rather than generic adjectives. For example, do NOT say: She wore a nice dress. Instead say: She wore a knee-length navy wool dress.

Rule #5: Limit your use of the pronoun I. Yes, a college application essay is about you. Yet dynamic language calls for reducing the number of times a writer uses the personal pronoun.

For example, do NOT say: I wanted to proofread the essay that I had written before I had to pick up my sister at her ballet lesson. Instead say: Before picking up my sister at her ballet lesson, I wanted to proofread my essay.

Rule #6: Vary your sentence length and structure. Be careful to avoid monotonous sentence structure that can lull a reader to sleep. Use some short and some long sentences.

Rule #7: Shorter paragraphs are easier on a reader's eyes. And you want the college admissions essay reader to actually read your essay. If you have a long block of text, break it in two or more paragraphs. Just be sure that each paragraph can stand on its own.

Sometimes a better editing choice would be to remove a sentence or two in a long paragraph. Many paragraphs of four or five sentences can have one sentence removed without losing any of the paragraph's meaning.

Conclusion:

And, remember, every time you make changes to your essay, you must run spell check and then read the essay aloud to check for incorrect words, missing words, extra words, or other errors that spell check might not catch.

After all, you have put so much effort into your college applications, you do not want to give up so close to the finish line.

Good luck!

If you found this book helpful, I hope you will consider writing a good review on Amazon at http://amzn.to/QWKFx8 as well as recommending the book via social media channels.

You can connect with me on Twitter at http://twitter.com/ZimblerMiller and check out my Amazon Author Central profile http://amazon.com/author/phylliszimblermiller and my Facebook Page www.facebook.com/phylliszimblermillerauthor

My nonfiction books on Kindle in the U.S.:

HOW TO SUCCEED IN COLLEGE AND PREP FOR BEYOND COLLEGE http://amzn.to/L2AGTQ

HOW TO SUCCEED BEYOND COLLEGE http://amzn.to/Mc13DT

TOP TIPS FOR HOW TO MARKET ON THE INTERNET WITH PICTURES: Action Steps You Can Do Immediately Whether You Are an Expert or a Novice http://amzn.to/Oa5Cmb

TOP TIPS FOR HOW TO MARKET YOUR BOOK ON AMAZON AND FACEBOOK: Action Steps You Can Do Immediately Whether You Are Traditionally Published or Self-Published http://amzn.to/N5H0Gj

My fiction books on Kindle in the U.S.:

CIA FALL GUY http://amzn.to/L38eiP

(continued)

LT. COMMANDER MOLLIE SANDERS (co-authored with Mitchell R. Miller) http://amzn.to/N6YyFZ

MRS. LIEUTENANT: A SHARON GOLD NOVEL (2008 Amazon Breakthrough Novel Award semifinalist) http://amzn.to/OXrBhh